Backbone.js Testing

Plan, architect, and develop tests for Backbone.js
applications using modern testing principles
and practices

Ryan Roemer

BIRMINGHAM - MUMBAI

Backbone.js Testing

First published: July 2013

Production Reference: 1050713

Published by Packt Publishing Ltd.
Livery Place
35 Livery Street
Birmingham B3 2PB, UK.

ISBN 978-1-78216-524-8

www.packtpub.com

Cover Image by Robin Chin Roemer (quiet.days@gmail.com)

Credits

Author
Ryan Roemer

Reviewers
Casey Foster
Jim Newbery

Acquisition Editor
Martin Bell

Commissioning Editor
Shreerang Deshpande

Technical Editor
Sumedh Patil

Copy Editors
Insiya Morbiwala
Alfida Paiva
Laxmi Subramanian

Project Coordinator
Sneha Modi

Proofreaders
Maria Gould
Paul Hindle

Indexer
Tejal Soni

Production Coordinator
Arvindkumar Gupta

Cover Work
Arvindkumar Gupta

About the Author

Ryan Roemer is the Director of Engineering at Curiosity Media, a language learning startup, where he manages technical operations and leads the development team. He develops (and tests) full-stack JavaScript applications and backend Node.js services. He also works with data mining, cloud architectures, and problems related to large scale distributed systems.

He was previously an engineer in the cloud computing storage group of Microsoft's Azure platform and most recently developed the search and cloud architecture for IP Street, a patent data mining startup. Besides engineering, he is a registered patent attorney (inactive), although it has been a long time since he has put on his lawyer hat.

You can find him online at http://loose-bits.com and on Twitter at https://twitter.com/ryan_roemer.

This book simply would not have been possible without the open source community, which has contributed to all the pieces of technology we have discussed in this book. In particular, the Backbone.js community's commitment to documentation, tutorials, and guides allows the rest of the Web to keep up with the amazingly rapid evolution of the Backbone.js library and ecosystem.

I would like to thank the JavaScript developer communities in the District of Columbia and Seattle, WA, for their incidental feedback, chats, and ideas throughout the development of the book. Additionally, I owe a debt of gratitude to the book's technical reviewers, as they put up with some quite rough early drafts of chapters, provided immensely useful feedback, and helped shepherd the book to its final form.

Finally, my most heartfelt thanks and love to my wife, Robin. Your support and help through the late nights, weekends, and a hectic cross-country move has been truly indispensible.

About the Reviewers

Casey Foster is a full-stack web developer born and raised in Southern California and now residing in Texas. He has been drawn towards web development since his early teens and has found a passion for JavaScript in the browser and on the server side with Node.js. He is a huge fan of open source projects and tries to open source as many of his projects as possible. He is a core contributor to the popular Backbone.js library and an active supporter of many other open source repositories. In early 2013, he co-authored his first book on Backbone.js, titled *Developing a Backbone.js Edge*. He can be found on GitHub and Twitter as `caseywebdev`.

> I would like to thank my wife Lacey and my puppy Gunner for their love and support in everything I do.

Jim Newbery is a web developer based in Edinburgh, Scotland, with a 17-year history of mostly building terrible websites and web applications. Once excited by being able to make text blink on a screen, he now spends his time working for the fantasy sports website `FanDuel.com`, tinkering with the usual plethora of half-finished side projects, and teaching his daughter how to make animated gifs of kittens.

> I'd like to thank all those developers that give up hours and hours of personal time to contribute to open source software projects that make my working life easier and more enjoyable. Thanks, in particular, go to Jeremy Ashkenas, TJ Holowaychuk, and Christian Johansen for creating the libraries and tools used in this book.

www.PacktPub.com

Support files, eBooks, discount offers and more

You might want to visit www.PacktPub.com for support files and downloads related to your book.

Did you know that Packt offers eBook versions of every book published, with PDF and ePub files available? You can upgrade to the eBook version at www.PacktPub.com and as a print book customer, you are entitled to a discount on the eBook copy. Get in touch with us at service@packtpub.com for more details.

At www.PacktPub.com, you can also read a collection of free technical articles, sign up for a range of free newsletters and receive exclusive discounts and offers on Packt books and eBooks.

http://PacktLib.PacktPub.com

Do you need instant solutions to your IT questions? PacktLib is Packt's online digital book library. Here, you can access, read and search across Packt's entire library of books.

Why Subscribe?

- Fully searchable across every book published by Packt
- Copy and paste, print and bookmark content
- On demand and accessible via web browser

Free Access for Packt account holders

If you have an account with Packt at www.PacktPub.com, you can use this to access PacktLib today and view nine entirely free books. Simply use your login credentials for immediate access.

Table of Contents

Preface

JavaScript web applications are soaring in popularity and driving exciting new application possibilities across the Internet. One of the most ubiquitous frameworks leading this charge is Backbone.js, which provides a modern and rational approach for organizing JavaScript applications.

At the same time, testing client-side JavaScript and Backbone.js applications remains a difficult and tedious undertaking. Even experienced developers can stumble across issues related to browser idiosyncrasies, complex DOM interactions, and asynchronous application behavior when writing frontend tests.

Backbone.js Testing brings sensible practices and current techniques to the challenges of Backbone.js test development. You will be introduced to fundamental testing concepts, a contemporary frontend test infrastructure, and practical exercises on all facets of Backbone.js application development. This book covers topics ranging from basic test suite creation to using test doubles to tackle even the most difficult/least testable Backbone.js application components.

With a little guidance from this book, you can test your Backbone.js web applications easily, quickly, and with confidence.

What this book covers

Chapter 1, Setting Up a Test Infrastructure, starts with the basics of how to set up your test application code and obtain the test libraries that we will use throughout this book. We create a basic test infrastructure, write the first tests, and review the test report results.

Chapter 2, Creating a Backbone.js Application Test Plan, begins with a refresher of Backbone.js fundamentals, introduces a sample web application for the book, and discusses a wide range of relevant testing and planning concepts. We conclude by writing and running our first Backbone.js application tests.

Chapter 3, Test Assertions, Specs, and Suites, covers the basics of writing Backbone.js test suites and specs with Mocha and test assertions with Chai.

Chapter 4, Test Spies, introduces the Sinon.JS test double library and how to spy on application method behaviors in Backbone.js tests.

Chapter 5, Test Stubs and Mocks, dives deeper into Sinon.JS, with stubs and mocks that can replace application method behaviors. We examine how stubs and mocks can reduce application dependencies in tests and facilitate easier and more tractable Backbone.js application tests.

Chapter 6, Automated Web Testing, enhances the test infrastructure built in the previous chapters to run automatically, for example, from the command line or a continuous integration server.

Who this book is for

This book is for JavaScript developers who are looking to create and implement test support for Backbone.js web applications. You should be comfortable with the JavaScript programming language and familiar with Backbone.js application development including the core components such as models, views, and routers, although you may be just learning the framework as you explore the testing topics of this book. Some exposure to testing methodology and technologies (in any language) would be helpful but not required.

Conventions

In this book, you will find a number of styles of text that distinguish between different kinds of information. Here are some examples of these styles, and an explanation of their meaning.

Code words in text, database table names, folder names, filenames, file extensions, pathnames, dummy URLs, user input, and Twitter handles are shown as follows: "We simulate slow tests using the native JavaScript function `setTimeout()`."

A block of code is set as follows:

```
describe("Test failures", function () {
  it("should fail on assertion", function () {
    expect("hi").to.equal("goodbye");
  });
});
```

When we wish to draw your attention to a particular part of a code block, the relevant lines or items are set in bold:

```
describe("Test failures", function () {
  it("should fail on assertion", function () {
    expect("hi").to.equal("goodbye");
  });
});
```

Any command line input or output is written as follows:

```
$ mocha-phantomjs chapters/05/test/test.html
```

New terms and **important words** are shown in bold. Words that you see on the screen, in menus or dialog boxes for example, appear in the text like this: "clicking the **Next** button moves you to the next screen".

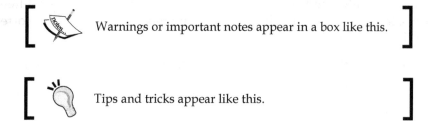

> Warnings or important notes appear in a box like this.

> Tips and tricks appear like this.

Reader feedback

Feedback from our readers is always welcome. Let us know what you think about this book—what you liked or may have disliked. Reader feedback is important for us to develop titles that you really get the most out of.

To send us general feedback, simply send an e-mail to feedback@packtpub.com, and mention the book title via the subject of your message.

If there is a topic that you have expertise in and you are interested in either writing or contributing to a book, see our author guide on www.packtpub.com/authors.

Customer support

Now that you are the proud owner of a Packt book, we have a number of things to help you to get the most from your purchase.

Downloading the example code

The source code for all the examples and files in this book are available at the GitHub repository (`https://github.com/ryan-roemer/backbone-testing/`) and introduced in more detail at `http://backbone-testing.com`. The `http://backbone-testing.com` website will always contain the most current and updated instructions for obtaining and using the code examples for this book.

 The code samples repository internally uses symbolic links for some libraries and files. Accordingly, Windows users may need to download the samples archive from Packt (see the ensuing instructions) instead of GitHub.

As this is an open source project, the examples may be periodically updated to fix bugs or to clarify code or concepts. Thus, the code snippets in the book may not exactly match the online code samples, but there should not be too much difference in practice. Ultimately, you can rely on the GitHub repository as the most correct version of the code in this book.

Due to limitations in the Chai assertion library, the minimum browser requirements for running the examples are as follows:

- **Chrome**: 7+
- **Safari**: 5+
- **Firefox**: 4+
- **Internet Explorer**: 9+

The vendor library versions that we use in this book include the following:

- **Backbone.js**: 1.0.0
- **Underscore.js**: 1.4.4
- **jQuery**: 2.0.2
- **Mocha**: 1.9.0
- **Chai**: 1.7.1
- **Sinon.JS**: 1.7.3

The GitHub repository will attempt to keep up with the changes as these libraries continue to evolve over time. At the same time, most of the application and testing samples in the book should continue to work well with the updated libraries for the foreseeable future, except where specifically noted otherwise in this book or on the website.

Files and code for each chapter are provided via a directory structure of `chapters/NUMBER`, where `NUMBER` is the chapter number. The example Backbone.js web application—Notes—is available in a `localStorage` version in the `notes` directory and as a full MongoDB-backed Node.js server in `notes-rest`.

To retrieve the example code, you can download the entire zipped archive from: `https://github.com/ryan-roemer/backbone-testing/archive/master.zip`. Another option is to use `git` to checkout the source code directly:

```
$ git clone https://github.com/ryan-roemer/backbone-testing.git
```

Finally, you can download the example code files for all Packt books you have purchased from your account at `http://www.packtpub.com`. If you have purchased this book elsewhere, you can visit `http://www.packtpub.com/support` and register to have the files e-mailed directly to you.

Errata

Although we have taken every care to ensure the accuracy of our content, mistakes do happen. If you find a mistake in one of our books—maybe a mistake in the text or the code—we would be grateful if you would report this to us. By doing so, you can save other readers from frustration and help us improve subsequent versions of this book. If you find any errata, please report them by visiting `http://www.packtpub.com/submit-errata`, selecting your book, clicking on the **errata submission form** link, and entering the details of your errata. Once your errata are verified, your submission will be accepted and the errata will be uploaded on our website, or added to any list of existing errata, under the Errata section of that title. Any existing errata can be viewed by selecting your title from `http://www.packtpub.com/support`.

Piracy

Piracy of copyright material on the Internet is an ongoing problem across all media. At Packt, we take the protection of our copyright and licenses very seriously. If you come across any illegal copies of our works, in any form, on the Internet, please provide us with the location address or website name immediately so that we can pursue a remedy.

Please contact us at copyright@packtpub.com with a link to the suspected pirated material.

We appreciate your help in protecting our authors, and our ability to bring you valuable content.

Questions

You can contact us at questions@packtpub.com if you are having a problem with any aspect of the book, and we will do our best to address it.

1
Setting Up a Test Infrastructure

Modern web development is witnessing a JavaScript renaissance, with the expanding popularity of frontend-driven, single-page, and real-time web applications. Leading and facilitating the charge are a number of JavaScript web frameworks that enable developers to sensibly organize frontend web applications into modular and convention-driven components. As more logic and functionality is pushed from the server to the browser, these frameworks are increasingly critical in maintaining single-page application state, avoiding unstructured and ad hoc "spaghetti" code, and providing abstractions and functionality for commonly encountered development situations.

This book will focus on one such framework—**Backbone.js** (`http://backbonejs.org/`)—that stands out from the crowd with a well-balanced feature set including small footprint size, solid core abstractions, and significant community support. Backbone.js provides a minimum set of useful interfaces (for example, models, collections, routers, and views) for application development while maintaining an enormous amount of flexibility with pluggable template engines, extensible events for cross-component communication, and a generally agnostic approach to code interaction and patterns. The framework is used at scale in applications for organizations such as USA Today, LinkedIn, Hulu, Foursquare, Disqus, and many others. Essentially, Backbone.js provides practical tools for data-driven, client-heavy web application development without getting too much in the way.

However, this evolving world of frontend development is scattered with many potential stumbling blocks. More specifically, while the theoretical application possibilities with modern JavaScript frameworks such as Backbone.js are endless, one of the most critical issues looming over rapid application development in this sphere is software quality and reliability.

JavaScript web applications are already notoriously difficult to verify and test: asynchronous DOM events and data requests are subject to timing issues and spurious failures, display behavior is difficult to isolate from application logic, and test suites depend on/interact with a specific browser. Frontend frameworks such as Backbone.js add another level of complexity with additional interfaces that need to be isolated and tested, large numbers of various small components interacting concurrently, and event logic propagating throughout application layers. Moreover, the implementation agnostic paradigm of Backbone.js produces wildly varying application code bases, making test guidelines and heuristics something of a moving target.

In this book, we will tackle the challenge of testing Backbone.js applications by identifying the parts of an application to be tested, asserting correct behavior of various components, and verifying that the program works as intended as an integrated whole. Kicking things off in this chapter, we will introduce a basic test infrastructure in the following parts:

- Designing a repository structure in which to develop Backbone.js applications and tests
- Getting the Mocha, Chai, and Sinon.JS test libraries
- Setting up and writing our first tests
- Running and assessing test results with the Mocha test reporter

We assume that the reader is already comfortable with JavaScript web application development and familiar with Backbone.js and its usual complements—**Underscore.js** (http://underscorejs.org/) and **jQuery** (http://jquery.com/). All other libraries and technologies will be properly introduced as they are used throughout this book.

 Although this book focuses on Backbone.js applications, the test techniques and technologies we introduce should easily carry over to other frontend JavaScript frameworks and web applications. There are a lot of great frameworks in the frontend ecosystem besides Backbone.js—try one of them!

Designing an application and test repository structure

Setting up a test infrastructure first requires a plan as to where all the parts and pieces will go. We will start with a simple directory structure for a code repository as follows:

```
app/
  index.html
  css/
  js/
    app/
    lib/

test/
  test.html
  js/
    lib/
    spec/
```

The `app/index.html` file contains the web application, while `test/test.html` provides the test driver page. Application and test libraries are respectively contained in the `app/js/` and `test/js/` directories.

> This is just one way to organize a Backbone.js application and tests. Other directory layouts may be more appropriate, and you should feel free to follow your own conventions and preferences in light of the specific development project at hand.

The Backbone.js application and component files (models, views, routers, and so on) are placed in `app/js/app/`, which may look something like the following:

```
app/js/app/
  app.js
  models/
    model-a.js
    ...
  views/
    view-a.js
    ...
  ...
```

The core application libraries are stored in `app/js/lib/`, which should include the libraries needed to drive the actual application:

```
app/js/lib/
  backbone.js
  jquery.js
  underscore.js
  ...
```

The test libraries and suites get a separate directory, `test/js/`, which isolates the test code from the application to avoid inadvertently introducing application dependencies on test functions or libraries:

```
test/js/
  lib/
    mocha.js
    mocha.css
    chai.js
    sinon.js
  spec/
    first.spec.js
    second.spec.js
    ...
```

Now that we have an abstract application and a test layout, we need to fill in all the pieces and populate directories with libraries, web pages, and test files.

Getting the test libraries

The ecosystem of frontend JavaScript test frameworks is quite rich, with libraries supporting different paradigms, features, and functionality. Choosing tools from this collection is a difficult task, without clear *correct* answers. In this book, we have settled on three complementary libraries, **Mocha**, **Chai**, and **Sinon.JS**, that provide an aggregate set of features particularly well suited for testing Backbone.js applications. In addition to these libraries, we will use the **PhantomJS** headless web browser to automate our test infrastructure and run tests from the command line.

Server-side JavaScript testing with Mocha, Chai, and Sinon.JS

Beyond the browser, JavaScript has seen a meteoric rise as a server technology via the immensely popular Node.js framework, supplanting traditional server-side languages and providing developers with a single-language web application stack. Although we will only discuss frontend testing in this book, the three core testing libraries we use are all available as server-side testing modules for Node.js. There are some non-trivial differences in integration and use (for example, Mocha reports are run from the command line and not a browser), but many of the general testing and application design concepts we will cover in this book equally apply to Node.js server applications, and you can conveniently use exactly the same test libraries in your frontend and backend development.

Following the repository structure discussed previously, we will download each of the test library files to the `test/js/lib/` directory. After this, we will be ready to write and run a test web page against the libraries. Note that although we pick specific library versions in this book to correspond with the downloadable examples code, we generally recommend using the most recent versions of these libraries.

Mocha

The Mocha (`http://visionmedia.github.io/mocha/`) framework supports test suites, specs, and multiple test paradigms. Some of the nifty features offered by Mocha include frontend and backend integration, versatile timeouts, slow test identification, and many different test reporters.

To run Mocha tests in a browser, we just need two files — `mocha.js` and `mocha.css`. For version 1.9.0, both these files are available from GitHub at the following locations:

- `https://raw.github.com/visionmedia/mocha/1.9.0/mocha.js`
- `https://raw.github.com/visionmedia/mocha/1.9.0/mocha.css`

At the time this book went to press, the most current versions of Mocha (1.10.0 and above) have introduced an incompatibility with the Mocha-PhantomJS automation tool that we will use later in this book. You can watch the Mocha (`https://github.com/visionmedia/mocha/issues/770`) and Mocha-PhantomJS (`https://github.com/metaskills/mocha-phantomjs/issues/58`) tickets for status updates and possible future fixes.

The JavaScript (`mocha.js`) file contains the library code and the CSS (`mocha.css`) file provides the styles for the HTML reporter page. With these files in place, we can organize our tests into suites and specs, run our tests, and get a usable report of test results.

Why Mocha?

Mocha is just one framework from an overall collection of great test libraries. Some of the strengths of the Mocha framework include solid asynchronous test support, server-side compatibility, alternative test interfaces, and flexible configurability. But, we could just as easily go with another test library.

As an example of an alternate framework, **Jasmine** (`http://pivotal.github.io/jasmine/`) from Pivotal Labs is another enormously popular JavaScript testing framework. It provides test suite and spec support, a built-in assertion library, and many more features (including test spies) — it is essentially an all-in-one framework. By contrast, Mocha is quite flexible, but you have to add additional components. For example, we leverage Chai for assertions and Sinon.JS for mocks and stubs in the test infrastructure of this book.

Chai

Chai (`http://chaijs.com/`) is a test assertion library that offers an extensive API, support for **Behavior-Driven Development (BDD)** and **Test-Driven Development** (TDD) test styles, and a growing plugin ecosystem. BDD and TDD will be introduced in more detail in *Chapter 2, Creating a Backbone.js Application Test Plan*. In particular, we will use Chai's chainable test functions to write assertions that read very closely to natural language, allowing tests to maximize comprehensibility while minimizing the need for explanatory code comments.

For integration, we need to download a single library file — `chai.js`. The version (1.7.1) that we want is available at `https://raw.github.com/chaijs/chai/1.7.1/chai.js`.

Alternatively, the current stable version of Chai can be found at `http://chaijs.com/chai.js`.

Sinon.JS

The Sinon.JS library (`http://sinonjs.org/`) provides a powerful suite of test spies, stubs, and mocks. **Spies** are functions that analyze and store information about an underlying function and can be used to verify historical behavior of the function under test. **Stubs** are spies that can replace a function with a different behavior more amenable to testing. **Mocks** spy on and stub functions as well as verify that certain behavior has occurred during test execution. We will explain these tools in more detail throughout this book.

In practice, Backbone.js applications comprise many different and constantly interacting parts, making our goal of testing isolated program components difficult. A mocking library such as Sinon.JS will allow us to separate testable application behaviors and focus on one thing (for example, a single view or a model) at a time.

Like Chai, we just need a single JavaScript file to use Sinon.JS in our tests. Versioned releases — we will use version 1.7.3 — are available at either of the following locations:

- `http://sinonjs.org/releases/sinon-1.7.3.js`
- `https://raw.github.com/cjohansen/Sinon.JS/v1.7.3/lib/sinon.js`

Installation of Sinon.JS, along with Mocha and Chai, completes the acquisition phase of our test infrastructure creation.

Setting up and writing our first tests

Now that we have the base test libraries, we can create a test driver web page that includes the application and test libraries, sets up and executes the tests, and displays a test report.

Downloading the example code

The source code for all snippets and code examples in this book is available online. Files and tests for each chapter can be found by number in the `chapters` directory. See the *Preface* for download locations and installation instructions.

The examples are best used as a helpful check on your own progress *after* a chapter has been finished and you have applied the lessons and exercises to your own code and applications. As a gentle admonition, we encourage you to resist the temptation to copy and paste code or files from the examples. The experience of writing and adapting the code on your own will allow you to better internalize and understand the testing concepts needed to become an adept Backbone.js tester.

The test driver page

A single web page is typically used to include the test and application code and drive all frontend tests. Accordingly, we can create a web page named `test.html` in the `chapters/01/test` directory of our repository starting with just a bit of HTML boilerplate—a title and `meta` attributes:

```html
<html>
  <head>
    <title>Backbone.js Tests</title>
    <meta http-equiv="Content-Type"
      content="text/html; charset=UTF-8">
    <meta http-equiv="X-UA-Compatible" content="IE=edge,chrome=1">
```

Then, we include the Mocha stylesheet for test reports and the Mocha, Chai, and Sinon.JS JavaScript libraries:

```html
<link rel="stylesheet" href="js/lib/mocha.css" />
<script src="js/lib/mocha.js"></script>
<script src="js/lib/chai.js"></script >
<script src="js/lib/sinon.js"></script>
```

Next, we prepare Mocha and Chai. Chai is configured to globally export the `expect` assertion function. Mocha is set up to use the `bdd` test interface and start tests on the `window.onload` event:

```html
<script>
  // Setup.
  var expect = chai.expect;
  mocha.setup("bdd");

  // Run tests on window load event.
  window.onload = function () {
    mocha.run();
  };
</script>
```

After the library configurations, we add in the test specs. Here we include a single test file (that we will create later) for the initial test run:

```html
<script src="js/spec/hello.spec.js"></script>
</head>
```

Finally, we include a div element that Mocha uses to generate the full HTML test report. Note that a common alternative practice is to place all the script include statements before the close body tag instead of within the head tag:

```
<body>
  <div id="mocha"></div>
</body>
</html>
```

And with that, we are ready to create some tests. Now, you could even open chapters/01/test/test.html in a browser to see what the test report looks like with an empty test suite.

Adding some tests

While test design and implementation is discussed in far more detail in subsequent chapters, it is sufficient to say that test development generally entails writing JavaScript test files, each containing some organized collection of test functions. Let's start with a single test file to preview the testing technology stack and give us some tests to run.

The test file chapters/01/test/js/spec/hello.spec.js creates a simple function (hello()) to test and implements a nested set of suites introducing a few Chai and Sinon.JS features. The function under test is about as simple as you can get:

```
window.hello = function () {
  return "Hello World";
};
```

The hello function should be contained in its own library file (perhaps hello.js) for inclusion in applications and tests. The code samples simply include it in the spec file for convenience.

The test code uses nested Mocha describe statements to create a test suite hierarchy. The test in the Chai suite uses expect to illustrate a simple assertion. The Sinon.JS suite's single test shows a test spy in action:

```
describe("Trying out the test libraries", function () {
  describe("Chai", function () {
    it("should be equal using 'expect'", function () {
      expect(hello()).to.equal("Hello World");
    });
  });

  describe("Sinon.JS", function () {
```

```
it("should report spy called", function () {
  var helloSpy = sinon.spy(window, 'hello');

  expect(helloSpy.called).to.be.false;
  hello();
  expect(helloSpy.called).to.be.true;
  hello.restore();
});
});
});
```

Not to worry if you do not fully understand the specifics of these tests and assertions at this point, as we will shortly cover everything in detail. The takeaway is that we now have a small collection of test suites with a set of specifications ready to be run.

Running and assessing test results

Now that all the necessary pieces are in place, it is time to run the tests and review the test report.

The first test report

Opening up the `chapters/01/test/test.html` file in any web browser will cause Mocha to run all of the included tests and produce a test report:

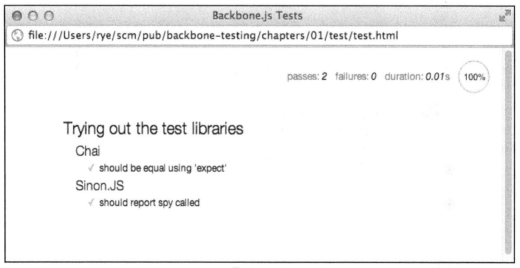

Test report

This report provides a useful summary of the test run. The top-right column shows that two tests passed, none failed, and the tests collectively took 0.01 seconds to run. The test suites declared in our `describe` statements are present as nested headings. Each test specification has a green checkmark next to the specification text, indicating that the test has passed.

Test report actions

The report page also provides tools for analyzing subsets of the entire test collection. Clicking on a suite heading such as **Trying out the test libraries** or **Chai** will re-run only the specifications under that heading.

Clicking on a specification text (for example, **should be equal using 'expect'**) will show the JavaScript code of the test. A filter button designated by a right triangle is located to the right of the specification text (it is somewhat difficult to see). Clicking the button re-runs the single test specification.

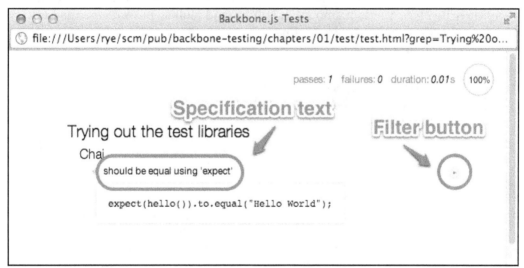

The test specification code and filter

The previous figure illustrates a report in which the filter button has been clicked. The test specification text in the figure has also been clicked, showing the JavaScript specification code.

Advanced test suite and specification filtering

The report suite and specification filters rely on Mocha's **grep** feature, which is exposed as a URL parameter in the test web page. Assuming that the report web page URL ends with something such as `chapters/01/test/test.html`, we can manually add a `grep` filter parameter accompanied with the text to match suite or specification names.

For example, if we want to filter on the term `spy`, we would navigate a browser to a comparable URL containing `chapters/01/test/test.html?grep=spy`, causing Mocha to run only the `should report spy called` specification from the `Sinon.JS` suite. It is worth playing around with various `grep` values to get the hang of matching just the suites or specifications that you want.

Test timing and slow tests

All of our tests so far have succeeded and run quickly, but real-world development necessarily involves a certain amount of failures and inefficiencies on the road to creating robust web applications. To this end, the Mocha reporter helps identify slow tests and analyze failures.

Why is test speed important?

Slow tests can indicate inefficient or even incorrect application code, which should be fixed to speed up the overall web application. Further, if a large collection of tests run too slow, developers will have implicit incentives to skip tests in development, leading to costly defect discovery later down the deployment pipeline.

Accordingly, it is a good testing practice to routinely diagnose and speed up the execution time of the entire test collection. Slow application code may be left up to the developer to fix, but most slow tests can be readily fixed with a combination of tools such as stubs and mocks as well as better test planning and isolation.

Let's explore some timing variations in action by creating `chapters/01/test/js/spec/timing.spec.js` with the following code:

```
describe("Test timing", function () {
  it("should be a fast test", function (done) {
    expect("hi").to.equal("hi");
    done();
  });

  it("should be a medium test", function (done) {
```

```
    setTimeout(function () {
      expect("hi").to.equal("hi");
      done();
    }, 40);
  });

  it("should be a slow test", function (done) {
    setTimeout(function () {
      expect("hi").to.equal("hi");
      done();
    }, 100);
  });

  it("should be a timeout failure", function (done) {
    setTimeout(function () {
      expect("hi").to.equal("hi");
      done();
    }, 2001);
  });
});
```

We use the native JavaScript `setTimeout()` function to simulate slow tests. To make the tests run asynchronously, we use the `done` test function parameter, which delays test completion until `done()` is called. Asynchronous tests will be explored in more detail in *Chapter 3, Test Assertions, Specs, and Suites*.

The first test has no delay before the test assertion and `done()` callback, the second adds 40 milliseconds of latency, the third adds 100 milliseconds, and the final test adds 2001 milliseconds. These delays will expose different timing results under the Mocha default configuration that reports a slow test at 75 milliseconds, a medium test at one half the slow threshold, and a failure for tests taking longer than 2 seconds.

Next, include the file in your test driver page (`chapters/01/test/test-timing.html` in the example code):

```html
<script src="js/spec/timing.spec.js"></script>
```

Now, on running the driver page, we get the following report:

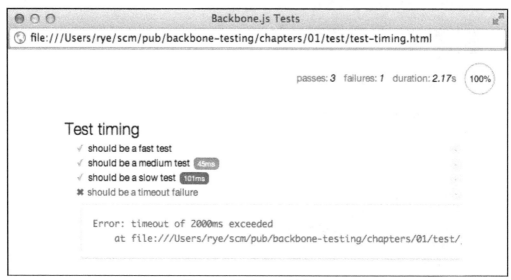

Test report timings and failures

This figure illustrates timing annotation boxes for our medium (orange) and slow (red) tests and a test failure/stack trace for the 2001-millisecond test. With these report features, we can easily identify the slow parts of our test infrastructure and use more advanced test techniques and application refactoring to execute the test collection efficiently and correctly.

Test failures

A test timeout is one type of test failure we can encounter in Mocha. Two other failures that merit a quick demonstration are assertion and exception failures. Let's try out both in a new file named `chapters/01/test/js/spec/failure.spec.js`:

```
// Configure Mocha to continue after first error to show
// both failure examples.
mocha.bail(false);

describe("Test failures", function () {
  it("should fail on assertion", function () {
    expect("hi").to.equal("goodbye");
  });

  it("should fail on unexpected exception", function () {
    throw new Error();
  });
});
```

The first test, `should fail on assertion`, is a Chai assertion failure, which Mocha neatly wraps up with the message `expected 'hi' to equal 'goodbye'`. The second test, `should fail on unexpected exception`, throws an unchecked exception that Mocha displays with a full stack trace.

> Stack traces on Chai assertion failures vary based on the browser. For example, in Chrome, no stack trace is displayed for the first assertion while one is shown in Safari. See the Chai documentation for configuration options that offer more control over stack traces.

Test failures

Mocha's failure reporting neatly illustrates what went wrong and where. Most importantly, Chai and Mocha report the most common case—a test assertion failure—in a very readable natural language format.

Summary

In this chapter, we introduced an application and test structure suitable for development, gathered the Mocha, Chai, and Sinon.JS libraries, and created some basic tests to get things started. Then, we reviewed some facets of the Mocha test reporter and watched various tests in action—passing, slow, timeouts, and failures.

In the next chapter, we will integrate a Backbone.js application as the target of our test framework and learn how to test, isolate, and verify program behavior throughout the course of application development.

2
Creating a Backbone.js Application Test Plan

Now that we have a basic test infrastructure, we'll turn our attention toward integrating a Backbone.js application and mapping out a test development strategy. In this chapter, we will create a test plan by working through the following topics:

- Reviewing some fundamental concepts of Backbone.js development

- Selecting a Backbone.js application to test

- Examining relevant testing concepts and approaches to guide test plan creation and execution

- Evaluating parts of the Backbone.js application to test in complete or partial isolation

- Identifying tests that exercise multiple interacting parts of the Backbone.js application

- Integrating the Backbone.js application into our test infrastructure, and authoring and running a few introductory application tests

A Backbone.js refresher

Although this book assumes a comfortable level of familiarity with Backbone.js, Underscore.js, and jQuery, we will briefly touch upon the basics of Backbone.js application development.

Backbone.js provides abstractions and useful functionality for architecting and developing JavaScript web applications. Backbone.js brings order to the chaotic interactions between program and display logic, DOM events, and backend communication. This is achieved via what could loosely be considered a **Model-View-Controller (MVC)** paradigm that separates application code into the following topics:

- Data modeling and retrieval

- Display rendering and user interactivity

- Brokering data and display logic to appropriately bind and manipulate data models and user interfaces

Backbone.js does not completely follow a traditional MVC approach, causing some observers to call it an **MV*** framework. An MV* application has a model and a view but has something other than a controller connecting the model and the view. For a much more detailed discussion on MVC and the various MV* approaches, see *Developing Backbone.js Applications* by *Addy Osmani*, and the article, *Journey Through The JavaScript MVC Jungle* (`http://coding.smashingmagazine.com/2012/07/27/journey-through-the-javascript-mvc-jungle/`).

To this end, Backbone.js provides a set of core library components:

- **Events**: The `Backbone.Events` module gives JavaScript objects the ability to emit and respond to events, including built-in Backbone.js class events as well as custom application events.

- **Models**: The `Backbone.Model` class provides a data wrapper that can synchronize with a backend, validate data changes, and emit events to other parts of a Backbone.js application. A model is the fundamental unit of data in a Backbone.js application.

- **Collections**: The `Backbone.Collection` class wraps a set of models in an ordered list. Collections provide events, backend synchronization, and many helper methods for manipulating and mutating the set of underlying models.

- **Templates**: Backbone.js leaves the choice of the template library up to the developer (we will use Underscore.js templates for this book). Other popular template alternatives include Handlebars (`http://handlebarsjs.com/`), Mustache (`https://github.com/janl/mustache.js/`), and EJS (`http://embeddedjs.com/`).

- **Views**: A `Backbone.View` object is the glue that binds models, collections, and templates together with the browser environment and DOM. Backbone.js is deliberately agnostic as to what a view must do, but a typical view references a collection or a model, couples data to the user interface via a template, and mediates user interaction and backend server events. To clarify potentially confusing terminologies, `Backbone.View` is much more analogous to a traditional MVC controller, and a Backbone.js template acts like an MVC view.

- **Routers**: Backbone.js programs are commonly developed as single-page applications in which the entire HTML page source and JavaScript libraries are downloaded in a single page load. `Backbone.Router` maintains the internal state of the application and manages the browser history. Routers provide client-side routing via URL hash fragments (`#app-page`) to allow different views to be linked to, bookmarked, and navigated like traditional web pages.

In the chapters that follow, we will test these components separately and together, so it is important to ensure a solid grasp of the fundamentals. The core documentation at `http://backbonejs.org` is a good starting point for the concepts, API, and pointers and tips on application development. For a deeper dive into Backbone.js topics, there are many great online and print resources, including:

- *Developing Backbone.js Applications* by *Addy Osmani*, which is a Creative-Commons-licensed book developed with the help of the open source community on GitHub. This book discusses the theory, architecture, and fundamentals of creating Backbone.js applications (`https://github.com/addyosmani/backbone-fundamentals`).

- *Derick Bailey's Blog*, which is a blog that is frequently updated with many Backbone.js posts and has been written by the creator of `Backbone.Marionette` (`http://lostechies.com/derickbailey/category/backbone/`).

- The official Backbone.js wiki page that aggregates blog posts, tutorials, and working examples (`https://github.com/documentcloud/backbone/wiki/Tutorials%2C-blog-posts-and-example-sites`).

Selecting a Backbone.js application to test

Devising and implementing a test plan is fundamentally a practical exercise, and we can better achieve our goal of overall application reliability by applying test lessons and techniques to a real application—whether it is one that has just been started or an existing application in need of better test coverage.

If you already have a Backbone.js application in development, you can most likely skip to the next section of this chapter. One potential issue we want to identify is the complexity of the existing application, especially one with minimal or no existing tests. Complicated dependencies, non-modular design, and highly coupled application components may require extensive mocking and stubbing to even permit a base level of test framework integration. Ultimately, the test infrastructure written around a legacy application will likely be quite different from the one written around a modular, decoupled application such as Notes. Accordingly, you may wish to use our reference application as a learning tool instead.

We provide a small reference Backbone.js application to use along with this book, simply named Notes. Notes is an online note manager that allows a user to create, view, and edit notes using the Markdown (`http://daringfireball.net/projects/markdown/`) language. You can try out an online demo of the application at `http://backbone-testing.com/notes/app/`.

The full source code of Notes is available as part of the examples repository (see the *Preface* for the download instructions). We actually provide two versions of the Notes application that share most of the same underlying code. They are as follows:

- **Local Application**: The `notes/` directory in the examples repository contains an application backed by HTML5 localStorage (`https://developer.mozilla.org/en-US/docs/DOM/Storage#localStorage`) for persistent, client-side storage in a web browser. The application can be run without a network connection from a URL based on `file://`, and will be used for most of the examples in this book.

- **Server Application**: The `notes-rest/` directory in the examples repository contains an application backed by a MongoDB database and served by a Node.js web server (available at `notes-rest/server.js`). The examples repository contains further instructions on installing and running the backend server.

Getting acquainted with the Notes application

The Notes application initially presents a user with a list of existing note titles with buttons for editing/deleting individual notes. The page also provides a **Write a new note** input form for creating notes and a simple search box for a user to filter displayed notes by title.

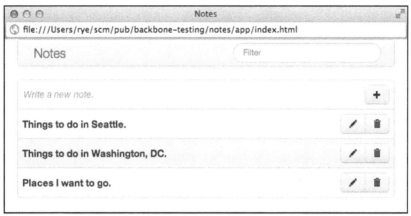

Notes list

Clicking on a note title, such as **Things to do in Washington, DC.**, activates the single note view and displays the note with rendered HTML (headings, bulleted lists, and so on):

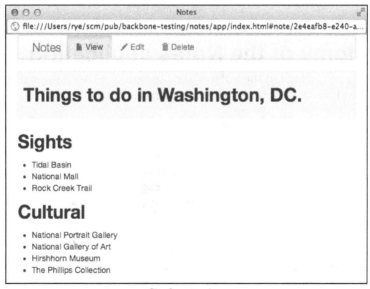

Single note view

The single note editor provides form inputs for title and Markdown text data. Any changes to the title or text are immediately saved to the backing datastore and made available for viewing:

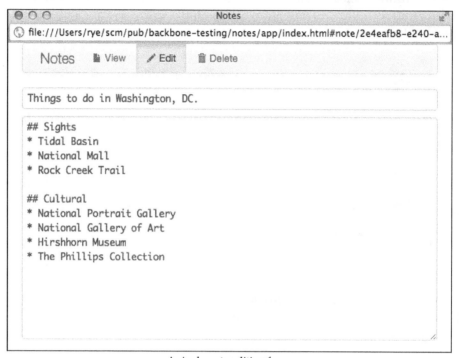

A single-note-editing form

The anatomy of the Notes application

The JavaScript `script` tags in the `notes/app/index.html` web page illustrate the program files and the overall structure of the application:

```html
<!-- JavaScript Core Libraries -->
<script src="js/lib/underscore.js"></script>
<script src="js/lib/jquery.js"></script>
<script src="js/lib/backbone.js"></script>
<script src="js/lib/backbone.localStorage.js"></script>
<script src="js/lib/bootstrap/js/bootstrap.js"></script>
<script src="js/lib/showdown/showdown.js"></script>

<!-- JavaScript Application Libraries -->
<script src="js/app/namespace.js"></script>
<script src="js/app/config.js"></script>
<script src="js/app/models/note.js"></script>
```

```html
<script src="js/app/collections/notes.js"></script>
<script src="js/app/templates/templates.js"></script>
<script src="js/app/views/note-nav.js"></script>
<script src="js/app/views/note-view.js"></script>
<script src="js/app/views/note.js"></script>
<script src="js/app/views/notes-item.js"></script>
<script src="js/app/views/notes-filter.js"></script>
<script src="js/app/views/notes.js"></script>
<script src="js/app/routers/router.js"></script>

<!-- Bootstrap and start application. -->
<script src="js/app/app.js"></script>
```

Don't worry if the long list of JavaScript libraries and application files looks foreboding. We will introduce each application piece as we test it. The examples in this book stand on their own without the need to look at the full source code of the Notes application. At the same time, downloading, running, and testing the Notes application is a useful exercise, particularly as you advance to the later chapters of this book and want to see the entire test collection put together in a single package.

Working our way through the JavaScript libraries, we start with the familiar core of Backbone.js (v1.0.0), Underscore.js (v1.4.4), and jQuery (v2.0.2). The additional vendor libraries in `notes/app/js/lib/` include:

- **Backbone.localStorage**: This allows us to save model data into the `localStorage` database for the `notes/app/` example application—`https://github.com/jeromegn/Backbone.localStorage`

- **Bootstrap**: This is a popular user interface layout and components library—`http://twitter.github.io/bootstrap/`

- **Showdown**: This converts Markdown text (for example, `## Heading`) to formatted HTML (for example, `<h2>Heading</h2>`)—`https://github.com/coreyti/showdown`

In terms of application structure and event flow, the key components of Notes can loosely be presented in a hierarchical fashion as follows:

```
app
  App.Routers.Router
    App.Views.Notes
      App.Views.NotesFilter
      App.Views.NotesItem
      App.Collections.Notes
```

```
App.Templates

App.Views.Note
    App.Views.NoteNav
    App.Views.NoteView
    App.Models.Note
    App.Templates
```

The application `app` bootstraps various application parts and starts up the router `App.Routers.Router`. The router routes hash fragments to either the list view `App.Views.Notes` or the single note view `App.Views.Note`. Both of these views use Underscore.js template strings from `App.Templates`. The list view `App.Views.Notes` contains two additional view objects for filtering and displaying list items, and a collection of notes. The `App.Views.Note` single note view contains two views objects for menu bar navigation actions and rendering Markup, and a note model.

Diving into the application files, the `notes/app/js/app/` directory decomposes into module groups, starting with some helper utilities:

- `namespace.js`: This sets up a global namespace for our application classes (`App`) and instance (`app`)
- `config.js`: This sets up configuration variables for the application instance, which we will be overriding in some of our tests

The application has a single model and collection that abstract the note data:

- `App.Models.Note` (`models/note.js`): This is a model class that represents a note
- `App.Collections.Notes` (`collections/notes.js`): This is a collection that wraps `App.Models.Note` model instances, representing a list of notes

All view templates are maintained in one file:

- `App.Templates` (`templates/templates.js`): This is an object literal that contains the Underscore.js template strings for rendering HTML sections for various views

The single note page has three view objects—a parent view (`App.Views.Note`) containing a child view (`App.Views.NoteView`) that renders a note, and a helper view (`App.Views.NoteNav`) for interacting with the navigation bar.

- `App.Views.NoteNav` (`views/note-nav.js`): This is a helper view that controls the note navigation bar options **View**, **Edit**, and **Delete** and listens for / triggers events for interaction with other views.

- App.Views.NoteView (views/note-view.js): This is a child view that renders note Markdown data as HTML.

- App.Views.Note (views/note.js): This is a parent view that represents a single App.Models.Note model for viewing, editing, and deleting. It contains the App.Views.NoteView child view and the App.Views.NoteNav helper view.

The list of notes on the home page has a similar assortment of views.

- App.Views.NotesFilter (views/notes-filter.js): This is a helper view for managing the filter form input and for hiding/showing notes based on the filter query

- App.Views.NotesItem (views/notes-item.js): This is a child view that renders a single note list entry on the home page

- App.Views.Notes (views/notes.js): This is a parent view containing an App.Collections.Notes collection, an App.Views.NotesFilter view, and multiple App.Views.NotesItem view instances, allowing a user to peruse available notes by title and click on action buttons to invoke specific note actions (for example, edit or delete)

Finally, we have the router and the application instance:

- App.Routers.Router (routers/router.js): This is the application router, which mediates routes for the home and single note pages.

- app.js: This is the Backbone.js application instance, which instantiates the App.Views.Notes and App.Routers.Router instances and starts routing history. The application instance is functionally similar to the main function entry point in languages such as C and Java.

These components serve as the basis for the test examples throughout this book. At the same time, the specific code, classes, and objects of the Notes application are not special or unique as a testing target—any Backbone.js application with a standard assortment of models, views, templates, and routers should suffice.

Numerous other sample Backbone.js applications are available as learning tools for testing and development practices, many of which are documented on the Backbone.js example sites wiki page. One particularly well-liked project is TodoMVC (http://todomvc.com/) that provides a simple task manager using Backbone.js. TodoMVC further provides examples of the same application using other JavaScript frameworks, including AngularJS, Knockout.js, Meteor, and Derby, making it a great way to try out popular frontend frameworks outside the world of Backbone.js.

Test paradigms and methods

There are numerous competing and complementary theories regarding software testing and development methodologies. Reading up on the world of test methods provides an excellent background for any developer looking to improve the ways in which they construct, implement, and manage tests. For brevity's sake, we will only introduce two paradigms in this book that are particularly useful for Backbone.js testing—Test-Driven Development (TDD) and Behavior-Driven Development (BDD).

Test-Driven Development is a process wherein tests are written first and *then* the actual code is written. The benefits of this approach include:

- Making tests a first-class priority in the development process
- Encouraging code to be written in small modular units
- Preventing the knowledge of code implementation details from unduly influencing the tests

TDD and general software testing principles are covered in many resources; a recommended reference on the subject is *Growing Object-Oriented Software, Guided by Tests* by *Steve Freeman and Nat Pryce* (`http://www.amazon.com/Growing-Object-Oriented-Software-Guided-Tests/dp/0321503627`).

 For the purpose of readability, we usually present the code first and the tests second. However, this is not necessarily the order in which the code and tests would be developed. Notwithstanding our examples, we strongly encourage that you incorporate TDD practices into your software development process.

Behavior-Driven Development is a refinement to TDD. It was developed by *Dan North* (`http://dannorth.net/introducing-bdd/`), and centers around specifying and describing tests in terms of the desired *behavior* of the application. In other words, BDD tests focus on what the *application* should be doing and not what the *test code* is testing, causing developers to ideally think less about internal test details and more about the application as a whole. To learn more about the principles and applications of BDD, a great starting point is the `http://behaviour-driven.org/` website.

BDD and TDD as library configuration options

The BDD and TDD paradigms are so prevalent in the testing vernacular that many test libraries have adopted the terms BDD or TDD to designate APIs and configurations. For example, in *Chapter 3, Test Assertions, Specs, and Suites*, we'll explore the Mocha bdd and tdd API interfaces. To avoid any confusion, it is best to view test library modes as just configuration options that may or may not have a strict relationship to the paradigms we have just discussed.

Testing concepts, approaches, and planning

Before jumping into the testing waters, it makes sense to have a plan of *what* we should test and *why*. The term **test plan** is heavily overloaded with many potential interpretations as processes, literature, and practices have been prevalent and continuously evolving for decades. It is not surprising that modern test plans can range from casual, mostly ad-hoc practices to formal, 100-page documents requiring executive sign offs at various stages.

For a more detailed discussion on the test plan practices applied to modern JavaScript applications, see the *JavaScript Testing Beginner's Guide* by *Yuxian Eugene Liang* (http://www.packtpub.com/javascript-testing-beginners-guide/book).

As Backbone.js applications are typically created in iterative development cycles, often without a lot of extra formality, we will take a fairly practical approach and create a test plan that simply identifies testing categories and applies them to the application under test. While an actual planning document or wiki is a best practice, it is not absolutely necessary. The overriding point is being able to identify what tests are appropriate for a given piece of code or feature during development.

We will focus on a few of the many overlapping concepts within the auspices of a test plan:

- **Unit tests**: Unit tests isolate parts of the application (individual functions, classes, and modules) to exercise. Some interpretations of a frontend unit test further require that the test executes quickly and without any I/O (network, disk, and so on).

- **Partial integration tests**: Integration tests typically involve testing the *entire* application stack—frontend, web server, backend datastore, and everything in between. We will not go that far in this book but will instead write frontend tests that combine multiple application parts (for example, collections and views) and verify that they are interacting correctly.

Unit tests take a narrow view and are often used by a developer to set forth a set of required behaviors for the small piece of code they are presently working on. Then, the code is developed to match up with the unit test assertions. Partial integration tests take a higher-level view, piecing together the application and checking that the individual components add up to a functional whole. In an exemplary Backbone.js application, a unit test might create a single model and test-only model methods. In contrast, a partial integration test might create a view with several subviews and a collection and verify that collection data changes modify the subview display.

Other concepts that we will not explicitly cover in this book, but that are worth becoming familiar with and integrating into the overall development and testing process, include:

- **Full integration tests**: Full integration tests incorporate the entire application (often seeded with known test data), exercise behavior as a user would through the frontend, and verify that the application responses propagate all the way from the backend to the user interface. For a Backbone.js application, this would entail pointing a browser window to the application's HTML page and running the application like a real user would.

- **Regression tests**: Regression tests isolate and expose reported bugs in an application. The tests are written *first* to verify that the bug is reproduced, after which the source code is fixed. The tests continue to be run as part of the overall test suite to ensure that the bug does not reappear.

- **Usability tests**: Usability testing encompasses many different forms and focuses on getting feedback that exposes portions of the application that need user interface or user experience improvements.

- **Performance/load tests**: Performance tests verify that the application maintains minimum response times for given use cases. Load testing checks that the application can still meet performance goals when different parts of the program are stressed.

- **Acceptance tests**: Acceptance tests form the criteria by which a customer can verify that the application meets its requirements. A suite of acceptance tests can include any of the categories of tests mentioned previously.

Now that we have had a brief introduction of these various testing concepts, we will develop an informal test plan for our Backbone.js application. We will examine the various parts of our Backbone.js application and identify what needs to be tested, what type of tests we should apply, and the behavior that we need to verify in the application. For the parts of an application that are still in development or in the early design phases, we'll go through the same exercises, just with a focus on the behaviors we expect the application to exhibit once it has been developed.

Testing individual Backbone.js components

Backbone.js applications are quite amenable to testing separation. Backbone.js provides a small number of core components that mostly avoid interdependencies. Our goal in this section is to identify the different parts of a Backbone.js application that can be unit tested in isolation and start thinking about the features of each one that we should test. Many components can simply be instantiated alone while others will need some extra mocking or patching help in our tests.

Models

Backbone.js models most often are independent entities that can be instantiated with a simple `new MyModel({foo: 123})` invocation. Accordingly, we can create standalone model objects in our tests without references to any other objects. Our model tests should include the assertions that:

- Objects can be instantiated with supplied and/or default values
- Data can be synchronized with a backing datastore (for example, `localStorage` or a REST server)
- Custom and built-in events fire and/or are consumed on appropriate state changes
- Validation logic accurately distinguishes the correctness of attribute data

Collections

Collections customarily have a single dependency on a model, declared like `model:` `MyModel` in the class definition. We can either directly instantiate collections in our tests or mock the `model` property for further test isolation. A typical set of collection specs should verify that:

- Collection objects can be created with or without an array of model objects
- Model objects can be added and removed from a collection
- Events are triggered on container and model changes
- Data is appropriately synchronized with the backend

Templates

Although templates are not an actual Backbone.js component, there are several conventional template development techniques for Backbone.js integration that we'll observe. Templates generally do not have any dependencies and can readily be used alone in test code.

The specifics of template tests largely depend on the engine used (for example, Underscore.js or Handlebars). A reasonable test starting point would confirm that:

- Template objects render the appropriate HTML output with the provided data
- Complex data structures such as arrays and objects are correctly interpolated in the template output

Views

Views frequently have the most dependencies of any Backbone.js component. Views can contain combinations of model, collection, template, router, and child/helper view references. Accordingly, we will have to mock or patch dependencies to isolate views and/or provide partial dependencies in our tests.

For all application views, we will want to verify that:

- Views can render the target HTML, binding model data to a template string
- View objects provided with an `el` property get added to the DOM on creation
- View methods correctly bind to DOM and Backbone.js events, and respond appropriately
- Objects contained by a view (for example, subviews and models) are properly disposed on the view removal

Routers

Routers commonly contain several top-level views and may have collection or model references. For unit-testing purposes, we will usually mock out dependencies to easily test the routing behavior without regard to the rest of the application. Our router tests will need to assert that:

- URL routes are accurately matched to appropriate views or other actions
- A router maintains the browser history correctly after navigation events

Utilities

Utilities include any helper code that is not actually a core Backbone.js class or object. As utilities are ad-hoc creations and have no real constraints, they can usually be unit tested easily, provided they are developed along with, and in consideration with, their supporting tests.

Testing application interactions and events

A Backbone.js application is used as a cohesive whole by end users, and wherever possible, we should have the test infrastructure verify overall application functionality and behaviors that cut across single Backbone.js components.

Partial integrations

While unit tests are a staple of modern software development, we must metaphorically move from unit-testing trees to the forest of partial integration tests to ensure that at least some pieces of the application work together harmoniously and reliably. In practice, this just means varying the degree to which we mock or remove component dependencies in the tests we discussed previously.

Integration tests can interact with application parts in many ways, including:

- By creating a parent view with a collection and subviews, invoking DOM events, and checking appropriate changes are made to both the collection data and subview displays
- By filling in and submitting the form input in a Backbone.js view
- By directly adding models to a collection and triggering events in listening views

Events

All Backbone.js classes extend the `Backbone.Events` base class and typically emit and consume events as a first-order means of communication. We will want to test that our application components trigger correctly and react to various expected events during the application's execution. We will often leverage tools, such as spies, stubs, and mocks, to exercise the event logic we want to test while not actually affecting other application states.

We will also need to carefully craft our test code to properly set up and tear down the test environment so that we can make reasonable assumptions about the starting event listener state in each test. For example, if multiple tests add custom listeners to a shared object without cleaning up, other tests could spuriously fail due to listener callback interaction.

The event behaviors that we will want to test across all our Backbone.js components include whether:

- Objects respond to custom/built-in events
- Objects emit events correctly
- Event listeners are properly cleaned up on disposal events, such as object or view removal

Dipping our toes in the application testing waters

Now that we can identify the aspects of the Backbone.js components that we want to test, let's begin planning and writing tests for the namespace utility and the Backbone.js model. For each component, we will examine application use cases and expected behaviors and then write tests to verify our expectations.

Namespace

The starting point for the Notes application is a namespace utility that provides two global variables to organize our application classes (`App`) and instance (`app`). In the `notes/app/js/app/namespace.js` example application file, we'll create the two namespace object literals with class/application properties:

```
// Class names.
var App = App    || {};
App.Config       || (App.Config = {});
```

```
App.Models       || (App.Models = {});
App.Collections  || (App.Collections = {});
App.Routers      || (App.Routers = {});
App.Views        || (App.Views = {});
App.Templates    || (App.Templates = {});

// Application instance.
var app = app || {};
```

The behavior that we want to test of these helper objects is if they contain the correct properties that other application components will rely upon. Accordingly, the chapters/02/test/js/spec/namespace.spec.js test file just needs a few specs to cover these objects. The first spec provides the 'App' object asserts that App is a JavaScript object with properties for all of the different grouping names (Models, Views, and so on) that we have attached:

```
describe('Namespace', function () {
  it("provides the 'App' object", function () {
    // Expect exists and is an object.
    expect(App).to.be.an("object");

    // Expect all namespace properties are present.
    expect(App).to.include.keys(
      "Config", "Collections", "Models",
      "Routers", "Templates", "Views"
    );
  });
```

The second spec provides the 'app' object just checks that the global app variable exists as an object:

```
  it("provides the 'app' object", function () {
    expect(app).to.be.an("object");
  });
});
```

Note model

Moving on to the actual Backbone.js classes, we will start with the model notes/app/js/app/models/note.js file that provides the data backing a single note in the Notes application:

```
App.Models.Note = Backbone.Model.extend({
  defaults: function () {
    return {
```

```
        title: "",
        text: "*Edit your note!*",
        createdAt: new Date()
      };
    }
  });
```

The model has three fields: `title`, `text`, and `createdAt`. As our example Notes application uses `localStorage` configured in the collection class, we do not have to provide backend synchronization declarations (for example, a `urlRoot` property or a `url` function) to persist model data. Because our model essentially comprises a single `defaults` declaration, the behavior that we need to test is simply that the default and modified attributes work as expected.

Our test file for the model, `chapters/02/test/js/spec/models/note.spec.js`, has two specs. The first spec creates an `App.Models.Note` object with default values and uses `get()` to verify each attribute:

```
describe("App.Models.Note", function () {
  it("has default values", function () {
    // Create empty note model.
    var model = new App.Models.Note();

    expect(model).to.be.ok;
    expect(model.get("title")).to.equal("");
    expect(model.get("text")).to.equal("*Edit your note!*");
    expect(model.get("createdAt")).to.be.a("Date");
  });
```

The second spec `sets passed attributes` tests a model created with the supplied values for `title` and `text`:

```
  it("sets passed attributes", function () {
    var model = new App.Models.Note({
      title: "Grocery List",
      text: "* Milk\n* Eggs\n*Coffee"
    });

    expect(model.get("title")).to.equal("Grocery List");
    expect(model.get("text")).to.equal("* Milk\n* Eggs\n*Coffee");
  });
});
```

Running the application tests

With our Backbone.js application files and the preliminary application tests ready, we need to integrate everything into the test driver we created in *Chapter 1, Setting Up a Test Infrastructure*. We will continue with the existing application directory structure by adding specs to `chapters/02/test/js/spec` and copying the application libraries from `notes/app/js/app` to `chapters/02/app/js/app`.

> The Notes application resides in the `notes/app` directory, which is the base location we will use to discuss the application components. At the same time, the chapter code examples are aimed to be independent. Therefore, we maintain our layout rules that the application code goes in `chapters/NUMBER/app` and the tests go in `chapters/NUMBER/test`.
>
> Accordingly, the downloadable examples link files such as `chapters/02/app/js/app/namespace.js` to `notes/app/js/app/namespace.js`. Thus, throughout this book, we will talk about a file such as `namespace.js` interchangeably using either of the full paths as a prefix.

In the `chapters/02/test/test.html` test driver page, we'll add `script` tags referencing our libraries, application files, and tests:

```
<!-- JavaScript Test Libraries. -->
<script src="js/lib/mocha.js"></script>
<script src="js/lib/chai.js"></script>
<script src="js/lib/sinon.js"></script>

<!-- JavaScript Core Libraries -->
<script src="../app/js/lib/underscore.js"></script>
<script src="../app/js/lib/jquery.js"></script>
<script src="../app/js/lib/backbone.js"></script>
<script src="../app/js/lib/backbone.localStorage.js"></script>
<script src="../app/js/lib/bootstrap/js/bootstrap.js"></script>
<script src="../app/js/lib/showdown/showdown.js"></script>

<!-- JavaScript Application Libraries -->
<script src="../app/js/app/namespace.js"></script>
<script src="../app/js/app/models/note.js"></script>

<!-- Set up Mocha and Chai -->
<script>
  var expect = chai.expect;
```

```
    mocha.setup("bdd");

    window.onload = function () {
      mocha.run();
    };
  </script>

  <!-- Include our specs. -->
  <script src="js/spec/namespace.spec.js"></script>
  <script src="js/spec/models/note.spec.js"></script>
```

The highlighted tag lines in the previous file illustrate that we have now added the core vendor libraries (Underscore.js, Backbone.js, and so on), the application libraries, and our two spec files. Opening `chapters/02/test/test.html` gives us our test report:

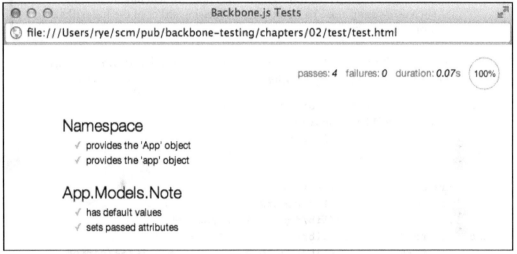

Test report

With our finished test report, we have now exercised and tested specific Backbone.js components and hooked everything into the overall test infrastructure.

Summary

In this chapter, we reviewed the basics of Backbone.js applications and introduced the Notes application as a helpful, if optional, companion to the test examples in this book. We then reviewed some relevant high-level testing concepts and dived into the specifics of what we will want to test in a Backbone.js application—in separated application pieces and as integrated parts of a whole. Finally, we wrote our first application unit tests and extended the test infrastructure from *Chapter 1, Setting Up a Test Infrastructure*, to execute our test reporter.

You should now be able to take an existing or in-development Backbone.js application, analyze its components, and create an abstract test infrastructure outline that will later be filled in with actual tests and suites.

In the next chapter, we will learn about Chai assertions, basic Mocha test constructs (specs and suites), test setup/teardown/configuration, and how to deterministically verify behavior in an asynchronous application environment. We will also broadly increase our test coverage as we write many more tests for our Backbone.js application in the course of learning testing technologies.

3
Test Assertions, Specs, and Suites

With a Backbone.js application integrated into our budding test infrastructure and a rough test plan underway, we will now begin expanding our application's test coverage. In this chapter, we will introduce some fundamental testing tools and test more parts of the Backbone.js application in the following topics:

- Surveying the Mocha and Chai test library interfaces and styles
- Introducing the Chai assertion library API
- Configuring the Mocha runner and the Backbone.js application for tests
- Aggregating Mocha specifications into test suites and preparing test state
- Writing test specifications in Mocha, beginning with Backbone.js collection specs
- Testing asynchronous application code
- Writing specs and HTML test fixtures for Backbone.js views
- Dealing with software/test development pitfalls and learning how to write testable code

Choosing a test style that fits

Mocha and Chai both provide different library interfaces for writing tests. This conveniently allows developers to choose an appropriate test paradigm or style for different projects while still leveraging the same underlying functionality.

Mocha test interfaces

Mocha currently offers four interfaces for test suites and specifications:

- The **Behavior-Driven Development (BDD)** interface: This interface uses test constructs similar to those popularized by the Ruby RSpec framework (http://rspec.info/).

- The **Test-Driven Development (TDD)** interface: This interface uses more traditional unit test keywords such as `suite` and `test`.

- The **exports** interface: This interface utilizes a modular format familiar to Node.js/CommonJS developers, implementing the test functionality as properties of a `module.exports` object.

- The **QUnit**-styled interface: This interface uses a flat declaration paradigm taken from the popular QUnit test framework (http://qunitjs.com/). A suite in this style is declared before and at the *same level* as a test instead of *containing* tests like the other interfaces just discussed.

Chai assertion styles

Chai provides two assertion styles:

- The **BDD** style: This style enables dot-notation chains of assertions such as `expect("foo").to.be.a("string").and.equal("foo")` using either the `expect` function or the `should` object prototype extension

- The **assert** style: This style uses single function assertions attached to the `assert` object, such as:

```
assert.isString("foo");
assert.strictEqual("foo", "foo");
```

Although `expect` and `assert` are functionally equivalent, there are some important differences between the BDD constructs `expect` and `should`. Essentially, because `should` patches the object prototype, it will not work for certain types of actual values (such as `null` and `undefined`) and is incompatible with Internet Explorer 9. For these reasons, our Chai BDD examples will use `expect` over `should`.

Trying out some different styles

Let's look at examples of the two most common interfaces for Mocha and Chai—BDD and TDD.

Mocha and Chai BDD interfaces

The Mocha BDD interface provides four main functional units:

- `before()`: This is a setup that occurs *once* before all the tests within a suite are run. Mocha also provides a `beforeEach()` function that runs before *each* test in a suite.

- `after()`: This is a setup that occurs *once* after all tests in a suite are run, with the `afterEach()` alternative that runs before *each* test.

- `describe()`: This specifies a test suite and can be nested within other `describe()` functions.

- `it()`: This defines a single test function containing one or more assertions.

Chai's BDD style uses `expect` or `should` to make dot-notation assertion chains.

We can create a basic test file `chapters/03/test/js/spec/bdd.spec.js`, which uses all of these components. We name the suite with `describe()`, add/remove a function with `before()`/`after()`, and test it with an `it()` specification declaration. We chain together two Chai assertions with an and helper, producing a composite assertion that reads naturally as "expect the result of `hello()` to be a string and equal to text 'hello world'":

```
describe("BDD example", function () {
  // Runs once before all tests start.
  before(function () {
    this.hello = function () {
      return "Hello world!";
    };
  });

  // Runs once when all tests finish.
  after(function () {
    this.hello = null;
  });

  it("should return expected string result", function () {
    expect(this.hello()).to
      .be.a("string").and
      .equal("Hello world!");
  });
});
```

Our test driver web page (`chapters/03/test/test-bdd.html` in the examples) adds the Chai `expect` function into the global namespace for convenience and configures Mocha to use the BDD style. The relevant configuration snippet is:

```
<script>
  var expect = chai.expect;
  mocha.setup("bdd");

  window.onload = function () {
    mocha.run();
  };
</script>

<script src="js/spec/bdd.spec.js"></script>
```

Mocha TDD and Chai assert styles

The Mocha TDD interface uses different names for the same basic units:

- `suiteSetup()` and `setup()`: These are aliases for `before()` and `beforeEach()`
- `suiteTeardown()` and `teardown()`: These are aliases for `after()` and `afterEach()`
- `suite()`: This specifies a test suite (`describe()` in BDD)
- `test()`: This defines a single test function (`test()` in BDD)

The Chai assert style is usually associated with TDD-style tests and provides an assert object with single function assertions.

Our TDD test file `chapters/03/test/js/test/tdd.js` provides the same test setup and assertion series as the BDD version:

```
suite("TDD example", function () {
  // Runs once before all tests start.
  suiteSetup(function () {
    this.hello = function () {
      return "Hello world!";
    };
  });

  // Runs once when all tests finish.
  suiteTeardown(function () {
    this.hello = null;
```

```
  });

  test("expected string result", function () {
    assert.isString(this.hello());
    assert.strictEqual(this.hello(), "Hello world!");
  });
});
```

The driver web page only differs in two configuration lines:

```
<script>
  var assert = chai.assert;
  mocha.setup("tdd");

  window.onload = function () {
    mocha.run();
  };
</script>

<script src="js/test/tdd.js"></script>
```

Opening up `chapters/03/test/test-tdd.html` in a browser should show exactly the same test results as the previous BDD example.

Deciding on the project style

The style options in Mocha and Chai offer developers a lot of flexibility in choosing test paradigms while still leveraging the same underlying test infrastructure. In this book we prefer the BDD style for both Mocha and Chai for a few reasons:

- Chai expect assertion chains read in a natural language format that often obviates the need for separate test comments

- The Mocha BDD interface components facilitate narrative descriptions of behaviors such as "this describes a number calculator" and "it should sum two numbers"

- The BDD interface is quite popular in the modern JavaScript testing ecosystem and encourages developers to describe the *behavior* of the code under test rather than to just identify the internal details

Nonetheless, if you prefer any of the other styles, please use whatever feels most natural. All of the test code examples in this book can be translated between the various Mocha and Chai interfaces.

A tour of the Chai assertion library

The Chai test library provides a robust set of assertions and helpers to aid the legibility and organization of tests.

Chai's own unit tests for `expect` (at `https://github.com/chaijs/chai/blob/master/test/expect.js`) provide a great starting point from which the API can be explored. Chai conveniently uses Mocha for its test framework (configured with the TDD interface). So the entire test suite should feel very familiar.

In this section, we will use a series of assertions to introduce most of the Chai BDD APIs. The assertion examples are accumulated into a single driver file for this chapter — `chapters/03/test/test-chai.html`.

 Chai provides aliases for many of the assertions that we will discuss in this section. For example, the deep equality assertion `eql` is also available as `eqls` and `deep.equal`. See the Chai API documentation for a full listing of aliases.

Chaining objects and assertions

Chai's BDD interface exposes objects that can be chained together to make test assertions more comprehensible. We will walk through some basic examples available in the file `chapters/03/test/js/spec/chai-chains.spec.js`.

As an introductory example, the assertion `expect("foo").to.be.a("string")` uses the chain objects `to` and `be`, which simply proxy through the eventual assertion. In this manner, Chai allows us to add any of the chain objects `to`, `be`, `been`, `is`, `that`, `and`, `have`, `with`, `at`, and `of` to form more naturally readable assertion statements. The statements `a` and `an` are available as both assertion chains and comparison functions.

We can use these statements to create language chain assertions such as:

```
expect("foo").a("string");
expect("foo").to.be.a("string");
expect("foo").to.have.been.a("string");
expect("foo").that.is.a("string");

// Chains can be repeated (or be nonsensical).
expect("foo").to.to.to.to.a("string");
expect("foo").and.with.at.of.a("string");
```

As all of the statements are equivalent, the highlighted language chains in the previous code demonstrate the many different ways of stating the same assertion.

Chai also provides language chain objects that *do* modify the ultimate assertion:

- not: This negates any following assertions. For example:

```
expect("foo").to.not.equal("bar");

// Let's get literary.
expect("Hamlet").to.be.not.to.be.an("object");
```

- deep: This sets the deep flag for equality checks. A raw equality check performs an identity test, which asserts that the two variables are the *same* object in the process memory. With the deep flag, Chai instead asserts that the two variables have the same property values, even if they are *different* underlying objects. For example, expect({foo: "bar"}).to.equal({foo: "bar"}) fails an object identity test while expect({foo: "bar"}).to.deep.equal({foo: "bar"}) succeeds.

Finally, most other Chai BDD assertion statements are chainable. The following example groups several assertion chains together with the and helper:

```
expect("foo")
  .to.be.a("string").and
  .to.equal("foo").and
  .to.have.length(3).and
  .to.match(/f[o]{2}/);
```

With these basic language chains and helpers, we have a foundation for writing readable assertion statements.

> It is a good practice to chain assertions together when it makes sense for the purpose of developer comprehension and writing concise and terse test code. At the same time, separate expect() statements can often be more appropriate.

Basic value assertions

Chai provides various assertion properties to check input values (see chapters/03/test/js/spec/chai-values.spec.js):

- ok: Value is truthy (for a quick introduction to JavaScript's permissive notion of conditional truth and equality, see http://www.sitepoint.com/javascript-truthy-falsy/)

```
expect("foo").to.be.ok;
expect(true).to.be.ok;
expect(false).to.not.be.ok;
```

- `exist`: Value is neither `null` nor `undefined`

```
expect(false).to.exist;
expect(null).to.not.exist;
expect(undefined).to.not.exist;
```

- `true`: Value is exactly `true`

```
expect("foo").to.not.be.true;
expect(true).to.be.true;
```

- `false`: Value is exactly `false`

```
expect("").to.not.be.false;
expect(false).to.be.false;
```

- `null`: Value is exactly `null`.

```
expect(null).to.be.null;
```

- `undefined`: Value is exactly `undefined`

```
expect(undefined).to.be.undefined;
expect(null).to.not.be.undefined;
```

- `arguments`: Value is the special JavaScript `arguments` object, which contains a list of parameters for the current function

```
expect(arguments).to.be.arguments;
expect([]).to.not.be.arguments;
```

Comparing values

Chai has a diverse array of comparison functions to assess input values (see `chapters/03/test/js/spec/chai-comparisons.spec.js`):

- `equal`: Strict (`===`) equality

```
expect("foo").to.equal("foo");
expect({foo: "bar"}).to.not.equal({foo: "bar"});
```

- `eql`: Deep equality—equivalent to `deep.equal`

```
expect("foo").to.eql("foo");
expect({foo: "bar"}).to.eql({foo: "bar"});
```

- `above`: The actual value is greater than the expected value

```
expect(1).to.not.be.above(1);
expect(5).to.be.above(2);
```

- `least`: The actual value is greater than or equal to the expected value

```
expect(1).to.be.at.least(1);
expect(5).to.be.at.least(2);
```

- `below`: The actual value is less than the expected value

```
expect(1).to.not.be.below(1);
expect(1).to.be.below(2);
```

- `most`: The actual value is less than or equal to the expected value

```
expect(1).to.be.at.most(1);
expect(1).to.be.at.most(2);
```

- `within`: The actual value is within the range of the expected values

```
expect(1).to.be.within(0, 2);
```

- `closeTo`: The actual value is within the delta of the expected value

```
expect(1.2).to.be.closeTo(1, 0.2);
expect(1.2).to.not.be.closeTo(1, 0.0);
```

- `match`: The actual string value is matched by the expected regular expression

```
expect("foo").to.match(/^f[o]+/);
```

- `string`: The actual string value contains the expected substring

```
expect("foo bar").to.have.string("foo");
```

- `satisfy`: The evaluator function takes the actual value as a parameter and returns `true` if the assertion should pass

```
expect(42).to.satisfy(function (value) {
  return value === 6 * 7;
});
```

Object and array validation

Chai provides some useful assertions tailored to objects and arrays (see `chapters/03/test/js/spec/chai-objects.spec.js`):

- `a`: When called as a function, this checks the object type building on JavaScript's native `typeof` test, with additional support for correctly inferring objects and arrays. Note that when `a` (or `an`) is used as an object property, it acts as a language chain instead.

```
expect("foo").is.a("string");
expect("foo").is.not.a("number");
expect({foo: "bar"}).is.an("object");
```

- `instanceof`: Checks whether the object is an instance of an expected constructor.

```
var Foo = function () {},
  Bar = function () {};

expect(new Foo()).is.an.instanceof(Foo);
expect(new Bar()).is.not.an.instanceof(Foo);
```

- `property`: Checks if an expected property exists in an object and, optionally, if the property's value matches an expected value. When used in conjunction with the `deep` language chain, an object structure can be navigated via the dot or array notation.

```
expect({foo: "bar"}).to.have.property("foo", "bar");

// Deep checking - object, and array.
expect({foo: {bar: "baz"}})
  .to.have.deep.property("foo.bar", "baz");
expect({foo: ["bar", "baz"]})
  .to.have.deep.property("foo[1]", "baz");
```

- `ownProperty`: Checks for the presence of a direct property on an object using the JavaScript `hasOwnProperty` test, without looking up the object's prototype chain for an inherited property.

```
expect({foo: "bar"}).to.have.ownProperty("foo");
```

- `length`: Checks the `length` property of an array or object (such as a string).

```
expect(["bar", "baz"]).to.have.length(2);
expect("foo").to.have.length(3);
```

- `contain`: Checks for the presence of an object in an array or a substring within a string. Note that `contain` (and `include`) can alternatively be used as a language chain with `keys`.

```
expect(["bar", "baz"]).to.contain("bar");
expect("foo").to.contain("f");
```

- `keys`: Checks that an object includes all of the expected property names. The assertion verifies only a subset of expected property names when combined with the `include` or `contain` language chains.

```
// Exact matching of all keys.
expect({foo: 1, bar: 2}).to.have.keys(["foo", "bar"]);

// Exclusion of any keys.
```

```
expect({foo: 1, bar: 2}).to.not.have.keys(["baz"]);

// Inclusion of some keys.
expect({foo: 1, bar: 2}).to.include.keys(["foo"]);
expect({foo: 1, bar: 2}).to.contain.keys(["bar"]);
```

Errors

Chai can also check abnormal code functionality, notably trapping and verifying program exceptions.

The `throw` assertion takes a function as an input that is expected to throw an exception when called. The resulting error is then matched against a constructor class (for example, `Error`) or a message string/regular expression (for example, `/message/`). Note that a function reference (for example, `bad`) is passed to the assertion rather than a called function (for example, `bad()`). This enables Chai to call the function internally, trap any exceptions, and verify the results:

```
var bad = function () {
  throw new Error("My error message");
};

expect(bad)
  .to.throw(Error).and
  .to.throw(/message/).and
  .not.to.throw("no message match");
```

Getting the application and tests ready to run

Now that we have the Chai assertion library API under our belts, it is time to write and organize the tests. While we have incidentally covered much of this material already, the concise core of a Mocha test infrastructure includes:

- **Test runner**: Configures the overall test run and report
- **Test suites**: One or more organization units grouping many specifications/tests
- **Setup/Teardown**: Setting up a state for each test or suite run
- **Specifications**: Writing the test functions

Starting at the highest level, we look at our test driver web page. As previously discussed, this is where our core application libraries, test libraries, and test specifications are set up and included. All of the Backbone.js application tests in the rest of this chapter are incorporated into the `chapters/03/test/test.html` driver page.

The Mocha test runner

The Mocha `setup()` function controls the overall parameters and environment for all test suite and specification executions. The function should be called once before execution starts (for example, `mocha.run()`) in the test driver web page:

```
mocha.setup("bdd");

window.onload = function () {
  mocha.run();
};
```

The default settings are quite usable for Backbone.js testing and we use the previous code for nearly all of the tests in this book. However, there are many more options available, which are described at `http://visionmedia.github.io/mocha/`. Here is an arbitrary sampling:

```
mocha.setup({
  ui: "bdd",           // BDD UI.
  reporter: "html",    // HTML reporter.
  timeout: 4000,       // 4s test timeout.
  slow: 1000           // A "slow" test is > 1s
});
```

Reconfiguring the application for testing

Backbone.js applications often need specific test-friendly configurations in order to make the test environment predictable and to avoid stomping on real data. Backend information (for example, host addresses and ports) is often different in the development and testing phases. Thus, it is a good practice to abstract all of this information into a common file so that we can easily switch values from one central location to another.

An alternative and complementary approach for creating a workable test environment is to fake out configuration details and dependencies with a library such as Sinon.JS. The two Sinon.JS abstractions that can help us here are stubs and mocks, both of which can replace object method behaviors during tests. (We will introduce and discuss these concepts in detail in *Chapter 5, Test Stubs and Mocks*.)

In the following datastore configuration examples, we could use a Sinon.JS stub to replace the entire datastore with test-specific simulation code. The stub would allow us to use normal application configurations while ensuring that we do not modify the real datastore. As an added benefit to this approach, stubbing and mocking external dependencies can often make tests run faster, particularly if the fake replaces a relatively slow application behavior (for example, network communication).

In the Notes application, we require a unique `localStorage` name for the collection, which we specify in the configuration file `notes/app/js/app/config.js`:

```
App.Config = _.extend(App.Config, {
  // Local Storage Name
  storeName: "notes"
});
```

This code populates the `App.Config` namespace with `App.Config.storeName`, which we then use for the `App.Collections.Notes` collection in `notes/app/js/app/collections/notes.js`:

```
App.Collections.Notes = Backbone.Collection.extend({
  model: App.Models.Note,

  // Sets the localStorage key for data storage.
  localStorage: new Backbone.LocalStorage(App.Config.storeName)
});
```

With this setup, the live application will save data to the `notes` store in `localStorage`. However, in our tests we will want to add, remove, and mutate the note data without overwriting our development-friendly datastore. So, by adding an extra configuration directive in our application's test driver page, we can set the test-only store name to `notes-test` using the Underscore.js `extend()` function:

```
<script src="../app/js/app/namespace.js"></script>
<script src="../app/js/app/config.js"></script>
<script>
  // Test overrides (before any app components).
  App.Config = _.extend(App.Config, {
    storeName: "notes-test" // localStorage for tests.
```

```
  });
</script>
<script src="../app/js/app/models/note.js"></script>
<script src="../app/js/app/collections/notes.js"></script>
```

By including `config.js` first and then overriding the specific values, we make the *other* unmodified configuration values available during the tests. With this scheme, we now have a completely separate Backbone.js test datastore, which we can change without affecting our development environment.

Organizing topics and specifications into test suites

Organizing test code into topics and application components is an important step in developing an overall test architecture. To this end, Mocha provides the `describe()` test suite function to group logical collections of test specifications.

For example, in `App.Collections.Notes` we might start with two subgroups of tests:

- Tests that create empty collections and verify the initial default state
- Tests that modify the collection with new `App.Models.Note` objects

Transforming this list into a set of nested Mocha test suites would give us:

```
describe("App.Collections.Notes", function () {

  describe("creation", function () {
    // Tests.
  });

  describe("modification", function () {
    // Tests.
  });
});
```

We have two levels of `describe()` statements here, although Mocha allows a much deeper nesting of suites.

Starting up and winding down tests

Although we try to isolate behavior for our test specifications as a general practice, tests often have common setup and teardown needs. For example, if a group of specs all test the same object, it may make the most sense to create the object once and share it with all of the specs.

Context/member variables in Mocha

Mocha allows test code to attach values to the `this` context object for use in other sections of the test run. This allows us to share variables across tests without having to declare and manage global or higher-level scoped variables. A common use of this feature is to add a variable such as `this.myCollection` in a `before()` setup statement for a group of tests and then remove it in the `after()` statement for the group.

Mocha provides the functions `before()`, `beforeEach()`, `after()`, and `afterEach()` to help us with test state management. As mentioned previously, the `before()`/ `after()` functions run *once* before and *once* after all the tests within a suite. The `beforeEach()`/`afterEach()` functions run before and after *each* test within a suite.

With these four constructs, we can create nuanced state management for our Mocha tests. The setup/teardown functions operate at the level of each test suite. This means that nested test suites can provide their own additional setup/teardown functions. For example, Mocha will faithfully run each `before()` statement as it traverses deeper into the `describe()` statements before executing the first test.

Another good reason to use the setup/teardown functions is that they *always* run—even when the test specs fail or throw exceptions. This prevents a single test failure from affecting the data state of other tests in the run and causing spurious test failures.

Backbone.js collection tests often benefit from using setup and teardown helpers to create an initial data state. Usually, this means adding some starting records (called data fixtures when loaded from a separate data file) and restoring the datastore to a pristine state after the tests have modified the collection.

In the test driver page, we have already configured the `App.Collections.Notes` class to use a test-only datastore. The `Backbone.localStorage` adapter has an internal method `_clear()` that clears the underlying browser storage associated with the collection, which we will use to reset our data state in the tests. The resulting data sandbox is ready for the following test scenario:

- Wipe any existing collection data on suite setup, add a context variable for a single collection, and remove the collection on teardown
- In the `modification` suite, add an initial `App.Models.Note` object to the collection and wipe the collection after each test

The implementation of the setup and teardown functions for the test suite looks like the following:

```
describe("App.Collections.Notes", function () {

  before(function () {
    // Create a reference for all internal suites/specs.
    this.notes = new App.Collections.Notes();

    // Use internal method to clear out existing data.
    this.notes.localStorage._clear();
  });

  after(function () {
    // Remove the reference.
    this.notes = null;
  });

  describe("creation", function () {
    // Tests.
  });

  describe("modification", function () {

    beforeEach(function () {
      // Load a pre-existing note.
      this.notes.create({
        title: "Test note #1",
        text: "A pre-existing note from beforeEach."
      });
    });

    afterEach(function () {
```

```
    // Wipe internal data and reset collection.
    this.notes.localStorage._clear();
    this.notes.reset();
  });

  // Tests.

  });
});
```

The highlighted lines in the previous code snippet illustrate the `before()`/`after()` calls for all tests in the overall test suite and the `beforeEach()`/`afterEach()` calls for only the subsuite `modification`.

Writing Mocha test specifications

With practically everything else in place, we finally turn to writing test specifications. Mocha BDD specifications are declared using the `it()` function with the following function signature:

```
it(description, callback);
```

The description string, by convention, is a statement of the expected behavior under test, and the callback function executes the tests. For example, assuming we have an empty `this.notes` collection variable, a test of the default values in `App.Collections.Notes` can be as simple as the following:

```
it("has default values", function () {
  expect(this.notes).to.be.ok;
  expect(this.notes).to.have.length(0);
});
```

Asynchronous behavior in tests

Although basic test specifications are quite simple, flow control complications arise when testing asynchronous application code. Given that the Backbone.js application's behavior is quite often asynchronous/event-driven, we need to have a solid and straightforward test approach.

Fortunately, Mocha provides an asynchronous test function parameter that is used to signal that the test is asynchronous. If a parameter is provided in a test callback (it is named `done` by convention), Mocha will delay the test completion until either `done` is called or the test times out.

One asynchronous behavior that we can test in a Backbone.js collection is that the `reset` event fires after a `fetch()` method call on the collection. Here we create an empty `App.Collections.Notes` object, fetch its backend data, and confirm that the event has fired. After all of this is verified, we add a call to `done()` to signal that the test has completed successfully. If the `reset` event never fires, then `done()` won't be called and the test will time out:

```
it("should be empty on fetch", function (done) {
  var notes = new App.Collections.Notes();

  // "reset" event fires on successful fetch().
  notes.once("reset", function () {
    expect(notes).to.have.length(0);

    // Async code has completed. Signal test is done.
    done();
  });

  notes.fetch({ reset: true });
});
```

With the extra `done` parameter, we can now run a series of asynchronous assertions within a single specification before the test completes.

Some Backbone.js collection tests

Now that we can write asynchronous specifications, we will finish off our test suite for the Notes collection. Keeping in mind our test goals for Backbone.js collections from *Chapter 2, Creating a Backbone.js Application Test Plan* (that is, modifying models, firing events, and synchronizing data), we will create the following specs for `App.Collections.Notes` (shown in an outline form here):

```
describe("App.Collections.Notes", function () {

  describe("creation", function () {
    it("has default values");
    it("should be empty on fetch");
  });

  describe("modification", function () {
    it("has a single note");
    it("can delete a note");
    it("can create a second note");
  });
});
```

Creating an empty test outline such as the previous code is a good exercise and practice during application development. For example, as part of a test-first development process, we can first write the `describe` and `it` declarations without callbacks to specify the world of program behavior for the relevant application component. Once we are satisfied that the outline approximates the expected use cases of the component, we can move on to filling out tests and writing the application code.

Helpfully, Mocha will treat spec declarations without functions (as shown in the previous code snippet) as pending tests. Pending specs are visually distinguished from the ordinary tests with different colors in a Mocha HTML test report. With pending tests, a developer can scan a test report more easily for unfinished specs and then implement the necessary test and application code.

With this in mind, let's implement the specifications to complete the test file `chapters/03/test/js/spec/collections/notes.spec.js`:

 We have omitted some of the spec functions from the following code (and elsewhere in this book) for brevity and readability. The full spec implementations for `App.Collections.Notes` and other Notes test suites are available in the companion code samples for this book.

```
describe("App.Collections.Notes", function () {

  before(function () {
    // Create a reference for all internal suites/specs.
    this.notes = new App.Collections.Notes();

    // Use internal method to clear out existing data.
    this.notes.localStorage._clear();
  });

  after(function () {
    // Remove the reference.
    this.notes = null;
  });

  describe("creation", function () {

    it("has default values", function () {
```

```
      expect(this.notes).to.be.ok;
      expect(this.notes).to.have.length(0);
    });

    it("should be empty on fetch", function (done) {
      // ... implemented in previous example ...
    });

  });

  describe("modification", function () {

    beforeEach(function () {
      // Load a pre-existing note.
      this.notes.create({
        title: "Test note #1",
        text: "A pre-existing note from beforeEach."
      });
    });

    afterEach(function () {
      // Wipe internal data and reset collection.
      this.notes.localStorage._clear();
      this.notes.reset();
    });

    it("has a single note", function (done) {
      var notes = this.notes, note;

      // After fetch.
      notes.once("reset", function () {
        expect(notes).to.have.length(1);

        // Check model attributes.
        note = notes.at(0);
        expect(note).to.be.ok;
        expect(note.get("title")).to.contain("#1");
        expect(note.get("text")).to.contain("pre-existing");

        done();
```

```
    });

    notes.fetch({ reset: true });
  });

  it("can delete a note", function (done) {
    var notes = this.notes, note;

    // After shift.
    notes.once("remove", function () {
      expect(notes).to.have.length(0);
      done();
    });

    // Remove and return first model.
    note = notes.shift();
    expect(note).to.be.ok;
  });

  it("can create a second note", function (done) {
    // ... omitted ...
  });

    });
  });
```

This final test file provides a reasonable skeleton using all of the different Mocha and Chai parts we have discussed in this chapter. We can see our tests in action by opening a browser to the driver page `chapters/03/test/test.html`.

Testing and supporting Backbone.js views

Having now created test suites for Backbone.js models and collections, we turn to expanding our test coverage to a Backbone.js view.

The Notes application single note view

The first Backbone.js view we will examine is `App.Views.NoteView`. This view is responsible for rendering `App.Models.Note` Markdown data into full HTML as shown in the following screenshot:

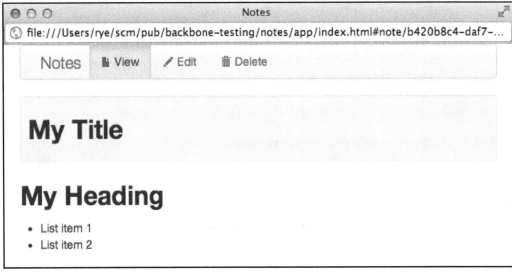

View rendered Markdown

The underlying model data for the figure includes the following attributes:

- `title:`

  My Title

- `text:`

  ## My Heading
  * List item 1
  * List item 2

The `text` attribute data transforms to HTML as:

```
<h2 id="myheading">My Heading</h2>
<ul>
  <li>List item 1</li>
  <li>List item 2</li>
</ul>
```

`App.Views.NoteView` is responsible for performing this conversion. The `notes/app/js/app/views/note-view.js` file first provides an `initialize` function, which sets model listeners to re-render or clean up the view and then kicks off `render()`. The `render` function uses the Showdown library to convert the model `text` Markdown data into HTML and then passes the finished data to the view template:

```
App.Views.NoteView = Backbone.View.extend({

    template: _.template(App.Templates["template-note-view"]),

    converter: new Showdown.converter(),

    initialize: function () {
      this.listenTo(this.model, "change", this.render);
      this.listenTo(this.model, "destroy", this.remove);
      this.render();
    },

    // Convert note data into Markdown.
    render: function () {
      this.$el.html(this.template({
        title: this.model.get("title"),
        text: this.converter.makeHtml(this.model.get("text"))
      }));
      return this;
    }
});
```

This view includes an Underscore.js template (`App.Templates["template-note-view"]` in `notes/app/js/app/templates/templates.js`), which inserts the `title` and `text` data into HTML:

```
App.Templates["template-note-view"] =
  "<div class=\"well well-small\">" +
  "   <h2 id=\"pane-title\"><%= title %></h2>" +
  "</div>" +
  "<div id=\"pane-text\"><%= text %></div>";
```

Rendering the model data into an HTML form with `App.Views.NoteView.render()` gives us the following resulting HTML:

```
<div class="well well-small">
  <h2 id="pane-title">My Title</h2>
</div>
<div id="pane-text">
```

```
    <h2 id="myheading">My Heading</h2>
    <ul>
      <li>List item 1</li>
      <li>List item 2</li>
    </ul>
</div>
```

Now that we have introduced a simple view to work with, we will examine how to test its behavior.

Creating HTML fixtures for view tests

The Backbone.js application tests that we have written up to this point don't interface with the DOM or HTML of a web page. This simplifies our test environment because the application's web page (for example, index.html) is very different from our test driver page (for example, test.html). However, Backbone.js views nearly always involve a healthy amount of DOM interaction.

To this end, we need an HTML test fixture—one or more DOM elements in the test driver page that we can interact with and modify during tests. At the same time, we don't want the fixture HTML causing havoc in the test code of the driver page. Accordingly, we create a single, hidden div element in the chapters/03/test/ test.html driver page for our application view tests:

```
<body>
  <div id="mocha"></div>

  <!-- Test Fixtures. -->
  <div id="fixtures"style="display: none; visibility: hidden;"></div>
```

Now, our tests can reference $("#fixtures") in jQuery and get access to the fixture container. The tests can then add elements as needed to exercise any desired view/ DOM interaction.

Advanced HTML fixtures

We have scratched only the surface of HTML fixtures in this chapter. More sophisticated fixture schemes and libraries exist, with features such as sandboxing application HTML code within an iframe to avoid test code cross-pollination and loading HTML fixture code from external application files. Two promising management libraries that are compatible with Mocha are jsFixtures (https://github.com/ kevindente/jsFixtures) and js-fixtures (https://github.com/ badunk/js-fixtures).

Walking through the view test suite

Let's make our way through the code in `chapters/03/test/js/spec/views/note-view.spec.js`, which is the test suite for `App.Views.NoteView`. Recalling the Backbone.js view testing goals in *Chapter 2, Creating a Backbone.js Application Test Plan*, we will check if the view renders appropriate HTML using a model and template, binds HTML results to the expected DOM location, and interacts correctly with the application events.

Writing tests on your own for the examples

To make the narrative in this book flow better, we will follow a general scheme of presenting a Backbone.js application component and then walking through tests that illustrate a particular lesson, technique, or tool. Unfortunately, this is the reverse of the recommended Test-Driven Development process, which writes tests describing application behavior first, then writes the implementation, and iterates until the overall behavior is correct.

For your work with this book, we strongly encourage you to take a moment, before the book presents test examples to design and implement your own tests for the sample application components. After writing your own tests, you can move on to the book's examples to check your work and identify additional testing ideas and techniques.

The suite begins with a `describe` declaration and a setup/teardown code. At the commencement of the suite execution, a view fixture (`$("<div id='note-view-fixture'></div>")`) is created and stored in `this.$fixture`. Our setup for each test (`beforeEach()`/`afterEach()`) binds the new `this.$fixture` fixture to the HTML fixture holder `$("#fixtures")` and creates an `App.Views.NoteView` object with an `App.Models.Note` model. After all tests in the suite are done, the fixtures holder `$("#fixtures")` is emptied:

```
describe("App.Views.NoteView", function () {

  before(function () {
    // Create test fixture.
    this.$fixture = $("<div id='note-view-fixture'></div>");
  });

  beforeEach(function () {
    // Empty out and rebind the fixture for each run.
    this.$fixture.empty().appendTo($("#fixtures"));

    // New default model and view for each test.
    //
```

```
    // Creation calls `render()`, so in tests we have an
    // *already rendered* view.
    this.view = new App.Views.NoteView({
      el: this.$fixture,
      model: new App.Models.Note()
    });
  });

  afterEach(function () {
    // Destroying the model also destroys the view.
    this.view.model.destroy();
  });

  after(function () {
    // Remove all subfixtures after test suite finishes.
    $("#fixtures").empty();
  });
```

With these variables and DOM elements available, we can test whether a default model renders the expected HTML, using jQuery. Note that because its `initialize` function calls `render`, instantiating an `App.Views.NoteView` object adds the rendered HTML to our DOM fixture:

```
  it("can render an empty note", function () {
    var $title = $("#pane-title"),
      $text = $("#pane-text");

    // Default to empty title in `h2` tag.
    expect($title.text()).to.equal("");
    expect($title.prop("tagName").toLowerCase()).to.equal("h2");

    // Have simple default message.
    expect($text.text()).to.equal("Edit your note!");
    expect($text.html()).to.contain("<p><em>Edit your note!</em></
p>");
  });
```

The second spec changes the model attributes `title` and `text` to render more complex HTML.

The tricky part is waiting until *after* the model listeners call `render()` and update the DOM to inspect the new HTML values. Our technique here is to observe that `render()` already listens to the model event `change` and add an additional one-time `once()` listener on this event to check the HTML.

However, note that this is a brittle way to handle the asynchronous nature of the test behavior. The rendering code could take more time to finish than our assertions, thereby breaking the test. A better solution is to wait on the `render()` function call to finish and then run the test code – a technique that we can more readily perform with Sinon.JS spies, stubs, and mocks, which are discussed in detail in the subsequent chapters:

```
it("can render more complicated markdown", function (done) {
  this.view.model.once("change", function () {
    var $title = $("#pane-title"),
      $text = $("#pane-text");

    // Our new (changed) title.
    expect($title.text()).to.equal("My Title");

    // Rendered Markdown with headings, list.
    expect($text.html())
      .to.contain("My Heading</h2>").and
      .to.contain("<ul>").and
      .to.contain("<li>List item 2</li>");

    done();
  });

  // Make our note a little more complex.
  this.view.model.set({
    title: "My Title",
    text: "## My Heading\n" +
          "* List item 1\n" +
          "* List item 2"
  });
});
});
```

Aggregating and running the application tests

Finishing up the test driver page for both the collection and view tests, we integrate the necessary script includes and HTML test fixtures in `chapters/03/test/test.html` (shown in the relevant part in the following code snippet):

```html
<head>
  <!-- ... snipped ... -->

  <!-- Test libraries. -->
  <script src="js/lib/mocha.js"></script>
  <script src="js/lib/chai.js"></script>
  <script src="js/lib/sinon.js"></script>

  <!-- JavaScript Core Libraries -->
  <script src="../app/js/lib/underscore.js"></script>
  <!-- ... snipped ... -->

  <!-- JavaScript Application Libraries -->
  <script src="../app/js/app/namespace.js"></script>
  <script src="../app/js/app/config.js"></script>
  <script>
    // Test overrides (before any app components).
    App.Config = _.extend(App.Config, {
      storeName: "notes-test" // localStorage for tests.
    });
  </script>
  <script src="../app/js/app/models/note.js"></script>
  <script src="../app/js/app/collections/notes.js"></script>
  <script src="../app/js/app/templates/templates.js"></script>
  <script src="../app/js/app/views/note-view.js"></script>

  <!-- Test Setup -->
  <script>
    var expect = chai.expect;
    mocha.setup("bdd");

    window.onload = function () {
      mocha.run();
    };
```

```
    </script>

    <!-- Tests. -->
    <script src="js/spec/collections/notes.spec.js"></script>
    <script src="js/spec/views/note-view.spec.js"></script>
  </head>
  <body>
    <div id="mocha"></div>

    <!-- Test Fixtures. -->
    <div id="fixtures"
        style="display: none; visibility: hidden;"></div>
  </body>
```

Opening a web browser to `chapters/03/test/test.html`, we can see the full test report for the collection and view:

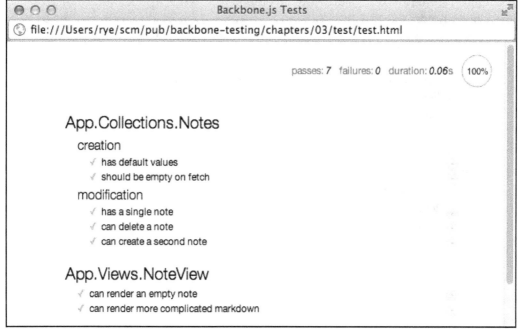

Test report

Test development tips, tricks, and hints

While we continue to explore the theory and practice of testing Backbone.js applications, it remains true that creating test architectures and writing good test specifications are more of an art than an exact science. Many lessons can only be learned through experience, particularly as your applications encounter bugs and development mishaps. In the meantime, we can start you off with some techniques and suggestions.

Isolating and excluding tests

Application development is a journey guaranteed to include inexplicable errors, sudden application crashes, and complex test failures. When these pitfalls happen, it is important to have some directions on how to debug the problems and move things forward.

A common scenario during software development is when application changes break one or more existing unit tests. In this case, a good practice is to run the test suite one test at a time, fix the test, and then move on to the rest. Mocha provides two avenues to help in this regard:

- **Grep**: As we have discussed in *Chapter 1, Setting Up a Test Infrastructure*, you can click on a single test in the test reporter HTML page or directly navigate to a test page URL with a grep query parameter appended, such as `test.html?grep=PATTERN`.

- **Only**: Another alternative is to temporarily modify your Mocha test specifications to run only a single test using the `only` helper, skipping all other tests and suites. Let's look at an example:

```
it("doesn't run this test", function () {
  expect(true).to.be.true;
});

it.only("runs this test", function () {
  expect(false).to.be.false;
});
```

On the other side of this scenario, sometimes we want to ignore a few failing tests while still using the rest of the test infrastructure. In this case, we look towards skip.

- **Skip**: The skip modifier omits a single specification from the test run and can be applied to multiple specifications. Skipped tests are also considered pending and can be visually distinguished in a Mocha HTML test report:

```
it.skip("doesn't run this test", function () {
  expect(true).to.be.true;
});

it("runs this test", function () {
  expect(false).to.be.false;
});
```

Writing testable application code

Beyond the practical aspects of writing tests, an equally important component of developing a test infrastructure is writing testable application code. The topic of testable JavaScript code is quite large—we will only introduce the issue here and start you off with a general goal of developing application code that works in harmony with the tests that support it.

A comprehensive treatment of the subject is available in the book *Testable JavaScript* by *Mark Ethan Trostler* (http://shop.oreilly.com/product/0636920024699. do), which covers topics such as application code complexity, event-based architectures, and debugging. Also consider general JavaScript application guides such as *Maintainable JavaScript* by *Nicholas Zakas* (http://shop.oreilly.com/product/0636920025245.do) and the seminal *JavaScript: The Good Parts* by *Douglas Crockford* (http://shop.oreilly.com/product/9780596517748.do).

Some Backbone.js application development hints and good practices for testable code include:

- **Decouple components and limit dependencies**: Many Backbone.js components have optional dependencies on other components. For example, a Backbone.js view can optionally have a model declared in the view class (for example, model: Foo) or a model object can be passed to a view on instantiation (for example, new View({model: foo})). The latter technique often opens up more opportunities for injecting mocks or test-friendly models into the view code. The same logic also applies to the el property in Backbone.js views—it is often more test-friendly to provide values via a view object instance than in the view class definition.

- **Isolate configuration information**: Any pure configuration data should get its own application file and facilitate the overriding of specific configurations. Canonical examples include the backend server host and port information, logging levels, and in the case of the Notes application, the name of the `localStorage` datastore. The previous examples that override `notes/app/js/app/config.js` provide a good introduction on how to both create a configuration file and supersede values for testing purposes.

- **Decompose large functions**: Monolithic functions that try to do everything are often difficult to test. Break up large functions into smaller ones, test them, and then aggregate the smaller functions into your application.

- **Avoid hidden state**: Using techniques such as closures and anonymous functions, JavaScript permits classes and code to have a state that is unchangeable and inaccessible to other parts of the application and tests. For example, if a class has an internal counter, make it a member variable and not a closure-wrapped variable. While this is something of a debated topic, it is generally preferred to expose some amount of internal state for test (and application) use. At the same time, our tests should focus on the application *behavior* and avoid deliberately using a internal state that is not part of the overall expected functioning of the application.

Please note that these tips are heuristics and not hard and fast rules. Many development situations will favor doing exactly the opposite of one or more of these suggestions. Hopefully, some of these guidelines will help make your early application decisions easier to live with as your application and test code bases grow over time.

Summary

In this chapter, we dug into the Chai and Mocha test frameworks, starting with a tour of testing interfaces. We explored the many assertion statements available in Chai, then examined the creation of full Mocha test suites with setup/teardown, application configuration, and test specifications for Backbone.js components. Finally, we reviewed debugging tips and guidelines for a more test-friendly software development lifecycle.

At this point, our application has starting test coverage for some Backbone.js models, collections, and views. We will continue covering different parts of our Backbone.js application while introducing new topics in the subsequent chapters and work up to a final application test collection that aggregates all of our work.

In the next chapter, we will get more familiar with the Sinon.JS library. We will use test spies to verify program behavior and introspect how functions are called and respond within a Backbone.js application.

4
Test Spies

As we begin looking at the more complicated parts of our Backbone.js application, the process of isolating dependencies and testable behaviors can become an increasingly daunting task. To provide a little help in these areas, we will introduce Sinon.JS, which is a powerful test mock, stub, and spy library, in this chapter.

Sinon.JS allows us to artificially isolate Backbone.js components and test specific behaviors without interacting with the rest of the application. We will kick off our discussion on Sinon.JS with the following topics:

- Identifying some of the test limitations typically found in Backbone.js applications and testing scenarios that can benefit from test fakes
- Introducing the Sinon.JS test double and assertion library
- Learning how to examine application behavior with test spies
- Integrating the Sinon-Chai plugin into Chai for better test assertions
- Testing Backbone.js application components with test spies and other Sinon.JS utilities

Fake it 'til you make it

Ideally, we would run insulated, fast, and consistent tests on all parts of a Backbone.js application without any modifications. In actuality, these goals encounter hurdles for at least some of the real code paths in a Backbone.js application.

We want to test Backbone.js components in *isolation*, but many components have dependencies on other parts of the application. We also want the tests to run *quickly*, but many parts of a Backbone.js application can slow things down, including the following:

- Network communication, such as persisting a model state to a remote backend datastore or a third party API

- Complex DOM manipulation with Backbone.js views and templates

- Timed events and DOM animations, especially those that deliberately wait (such as a slow jQuery fade)

Finally, many events and execution paths in a Backbone.js application are non-deterministic. For example, parallel network requests and user inputs can be received by the application in any order. To deal with these issues, we sometimes have to look beyond the actual program code and fake out some parts of the application during tests. For a deeper dive into some of the common testing limitations and motivations for faking, see *Planning, Cheating and Faking Your Way Through JavaScript Tests* by *Christian Johansen* (the creator of Sinon.JS) at http://msdn.microsoft.com/en-us/magazine/gg649850.aspx.

The modern techniques used to observe and/or replace program behaviors are collectively dubbed **test doubles**. The test doubles that we use in this book include:

- **Spies**: A test spy wraps a method under test and records inputs and outputs for later use. However, it does not change any of the underlying method functionality, as a spy is merely an observer. Test spies are useful in situations where we want to check how and when a given function is called from other parts of the application.

- **Stubs**: A test stub is a spy that additionally replaces the functionality of a method under test with a new behavior. Stubs are quite useful for test isolation. For example, when testing a single method that normally calls other functions, we can simply "stub out" the external function calls with a preprogrammed behavior. In this manner, tests can execute the specific code under test while faking out everything else.

- **Mocks**: Mocks are a combination of spies and stubs (observing function calls and replacing function behavior) that additionally verify expected function behavior during execution.

For a good survey on test doubles, including approaches beyond the three we identified, see *Exploring The Continuum Of Test Doubles* by *Mark Seeman* (http://msdn.microsoft.com/en-us/magazine/cc163358.aspx) and *Test Double Patterns* web page by *Gerard Meszaros* (http://xunitpatterns.com/Test%20Double%20Patterns.html).

Getting to know Sinon.JS

Sinon.JS is a popular test double library that provides spies, stubs, mocks, fake servers, and various helpers. We will introduce two Sinon.JS interfaces in this chapter — spies and the sandboxed test helper — and discuss the rest in *Chapter 5, Test Stubs and Mocks*.

Spying on functions with Sinon.JS

Sinon.JS provides extensible test spies that can record many different aspects of a function execution, including calling parameters, return values, and thrown exceptions. The basic developer workflow is to create a spy, hook it into a function under test, execute the function, and then verify that the spy's recorded information matches with the test expectations. In this section, we will walk through the different ways to create spies and discuss some of the most useful parts of the Sinon.JS spy API.

Anonymous spies

Spies can be created as anonymous standalone functions, which are often used to test event logic in Backbone.js applications. For example, we create a Backbone.js event object and an anonymous Sinon.JS spy in the following code. The spy listens to the foo event, which we trigger. Then, we can inspect the spy and assert that the spy was called once and passed 42 as a parameter:

```
it("calls anonymous spy on event", function () {
  var eventer = _.extend({}, Backbone.Events),
    spy = sinon.spy();

  // Set up the spy.
  eventer.on("foo", spy);
  expect(spy.called).to.be.false;

  // Fire event.
  eventer.trigger("foo", 42);

  // Check number of calls.
```

```
      expect(spy.calledOnce).to.be.true;
      expect(spy.callCount).to.equal(1);

      // Check calling arguments.
      expect(spy.firstCall.args[0]).to.equal(42);
      expect(spy.calledWith(42)).to.be.true;
    });
```

Spy assertions

Sinon.JS provides assertion helpers for many spy methods and properties with the `sinon.assert` object. In the previous example, we used Chai assertions to verify the spy's recorded information. But, we could have equivalently used Sinon.JS assertions as follows:

```
    it("verifies anonymous spy on event", function () {
      var eventer = _.extend({}, Backbone.Events),
        spy = sinon.spy();

      eventer.on("foo", spy);
      sinon.assert.notCalled(spy);

      eventer.trigger("foo", 42);
      sinon.assert.callCount(spy, 1);
      sinon.assert.calledWith(spy, 42);
    });
```

The `sinon.assert` helpers have an advantage over most equivalent Chai assertions for the reason that the failure messages are informative and specific. For example, a failing assertion for `sinon.assert.calledWith(spy, 42)` produces the error message `AssertError: expected spy to be called with arguments 42`.

Function spies

Sinon.JS spies can wrap existing functions as well. In the following example, we wrap the function `divide` with a spy, producing `divAndSpy`. Then, we can call `divAndSpy` in any manner that we could for `divide`. We can also inspect spy properties such as `calledWith()` in the wrapped spy:

```
    it("calls spy wrapper on function", function () {
      var divide = function (a, b) { return a / b; },
        divAndSpy = sinon.spy(divide);

      // Call wrapped function and verify result.
```

```
expect(divAndSpy(4, 2)).to.equal(2);

// Now, verify spy properties.
sinon.assert.calledOnce(divAndSpy);
sinon.assert.calledWith(divAndSpy, 4, 2);

// Sinon.JS doesn't have assert for returned.
expect(divAndSpy.returned(2)).to.be.true;
});
```

Object method spies

Finally, Sinon.JS spies can wrap methods in objects. This is a particularly powerful means of spying on one method within an overall class or Backbone.js component to gather information throughout the entire execution path. The wrapped object methods contain Sinon.JS spy properties, meaning that we do not have to separately track a spy variable.

Wrapped object methods remain spies until unwrapped with the restore() function, which removes the spy and reinstates the original function. As an example, let us consider the following object with two methods:

```
var obj = {
  multiply: function (a, b) { return a * b; },
  error: function (msg) { throw new Error(msg); }
};
```

We can spy on multiply to verify its call and return values, and spy on error to check that it throws an expected exception. In both cases, we call the wrapped object method directly (for example, obj.multiply()) and then access the method spies. Finally, we need to call restore() at the end of the test to unwrap the spies on obj:

```
it("calls spy on wrapped object", function () {
  // Wrap members with `sinon` directly.
  sinon.spy(obj, "multiply");
  sinon.spy(obj, "error");

  expect(obj.multiply(5, 2)).to.equal(10);
  sinon.assert.calledWith(obj.multiply, 5, 2);
  expect(obj.multiply.returned(10)).to.be.true;

  try {
    obj.error("Foo");
  } catch (e) {}
```

```
sinon.assert.threw(obj.error, "Error");

// Have to restore after tests finish.
obj.multiply.restore();
obj.error.restore();
});
```

Playing in the sandbox with Sinon.JS test helpers

One issue with the previous example spec is that if an assertion fails before restore() is called, the object methods are still wrapped in the spies. If any subsequent (and otherwise passing) test tries to wrap an already wrapped method, Sinon.JS will throw an error such as TypeError: Attempted to wrap <function name> which is already wrapped.

Thus, it is important to ensure that each spy eventually calls restore(), regardless of whether or not the underlying test has passed. One way of achieving this is with a try/finally block in the test. Another way is to create spies in a before function and call restore() on them in an after function. However, the easiest and the most flexible way is to perhaps use the sinon.test sandbox function.

Sinon.JS provides an execution environment dubbed as a **sandbox** that can be configured with spies, stubs, mocks, and other fake objects (for example, fake timers and AJAX requests). Conveniently, all faked properties and methods can be unwound with a single restore() call on the sandbox object.

 Reviewing the Sinon.JS sandbox documentation at http://sinonjs. org/docs/#sandbox is highly recommended. There are some subtle pitfalls and surprises related to how an application execution changes within a sandbox. For example, the default sandbox will fake time and the related functions such as setTimeout. It means that if your code waits for 10 milliseconds before execution, it will not run until the developer *manually* advances the time in the fake clock object.

The sinon.test wrapper function takes this one step further by creating a default sandbox, which is automatically restored after the wrapped code finishes its execution. Repeating our previous object method example with sinon.test yields a more elegant version of the spec, in which we don't manually call restore() on the spies and still guarantee that the wrapped object methods are restored:

```
it("calls spy with test helper", sinon.test(function () {
    // Wrap members using context (`this`) helper.
    this.spy(obj, "multiply");
```

```
this.spy(obj, "error");

expect(obj.multiply(5, 2)).to.equal(10);
sinon.assert.calledWith(obj.multiply, 5, 2);
expect(obj.multiply.returned(10)).to.be.true;

try {
  obj.error("Foo");
} catch (e) {}
sinon.assert.threw(obj.error, "Error");

// No restore is necessary.
}));
```

While the `sinon.test` helper is a handy tool for managing Sinon.JS objects, it is not always an appropriate choice for every spec. For example, asynchronous Mocha tests are tricky because `sinon.test` can potentially restore the entire sandbox before the `done()` parameter is later called in the test code. Additionally, a side effect of using `sinon.test` is that the Mocha test reporter will no longer show the test code when clicking on a spec description in the test driver web page. The reason for this makes sense — `sinon.test` wraps the actual test function, so `sinon.test` is all that the Mocha reporter sees. It is ultimately a matter of developer intuition and experience as to when to use the `sinon.test` shortcut. In this book we use the wrapper for a subset of our synchronous Sinon.JS-based specs.

Delving into the Sinon.JS spy API

Sinon.JS spies provide a fairly comprehensive set of properties and methods for inspecting execution information (see `http://sinonjs.org/docs/#spies` for a complete list). Spies can be inspected *generally* to see if an argument or return value was ever encountered during execution or *specifically* to check information for a single function call.

The spy API

An introductory set of useful spy methods and properties includes:

- `spy.callCount(num)`: This returns the number of times the spied function was called. This is available as an assertion with `sinon.assert.callCount(spy, num)`.

- spy.called: This is true if the function was called one or more times. Sinon.JS also provides properties to verify a few specific call counts, for example, spy.calledOnce. Assertion versions include sinon.assert. called(spy), sinon.assert.notCalled(spy), and sinon.assert. calledOnce(spy).

- spy.calledWith*/spy.notCalledWith*: Sinon.JS provides methods that can verify if a spy was sometimes/always called with expected parameters. For example, spy.calledWithExactly(arg1, arg2) checks whether the function was called one or more times with arg1 and arg2. By contrast, spy. alwaysCalledWith(arg1) checks whether every function call had a first argument arg1 and any number of additional arguments.

- spy.returned(obj)/spy.alwaysReturned(obj): This returns true if obj was returned by the function one or more times/on every call.

Sinon.js spies also record thrown exceptions, which can be inspected with the following methods:

- spy.threw(): This returns true if the function threw an exception one or more times. The spy.alwaysThrew() alternative returns true if the exception was thrown every time. Both can take optional arguments of the type string (for example, "Error") or an actual error object to additionally require a type match for the exception. Assertion versions are sinon. assert.threw(spy) and sinon.assert.alwaysThrew(spy) respectively.

The spy call API

Each time a spied function is called, Sinon.JS stores a **call object** with relevant information in an internal array. Call objects are useful in situations where a spied function is executed many times, but only one specific call needs to be inspected.

Call objects can be accessed from a spy in various ways:

- spy.getCall(n): Retrieves the *n*th call object of the spy from a zero-indexed array. For example, spy.getCall(1) retrieves the call object from the second time the spied function was called.

- spy.firstCall, spy.secondCall, spy.thirdCall, and spy.lastCall: These are helper properties that access commonly used call objects.

Call objects provide methods and properties for the particular function call they wrap:

- `spyCall.calledOn(obj)`: This returns `true` if `obj` was the context (`this`) variable for the call. The `this` variable's value is also available directly from the property `spyCall.thisValue`.

- `spyCall.calledWith*`/`spyCall.notCalledWith*`: These are spy call methods that verify if a *single* call was/was not made with specific arguments. It parallels the spy API methods, which instead check *all* the function calls and not just one. The call object also provides the specific arguments the function was called with, in the property `spyCall.args`.

- `spyCall.returnValue`: This is the property containing the return value for the function call.

- `spyCall.threw()`: This returns `true` if the function call threw an exception. The exception object itself is available as `spyCall.exception`.

Spicing up Chai with the Sinon.JS plugin

One of the primary motivations for using the Chai library is the natural language syntax of its chained assertions. Another strong point of Chai is that it produces clear error messages on assertion failures.

Unfortunately, Sinon.JS spies create some assertion challenges within our test framework. To illustrate the issue, let's focus on the previous example that asserts that the `obj.multiply()` method (wrapped in a spy) was called with the parameters 5 and 2.

At this point, we have encountered two ways of making assertions on Sinon.JS spies—with Chai assertions and with Sinon.JS built-in spy assertions. Starting with the first method, we can write a Chai assertion on the spy as follows:

```
expect(obj.multiply.calledWith(5, 2)).to.be.true;
```

However, a drawback of this statement is that if the assertion fails, Chai will produce the unhelpful error message `expected false to be true`.

We can get a much better error message, `AssertError: expected multiply to be called with arguments 5, 2`, if we use the Sinon.JS assert version:

```
sinon.assert.calledWith(obj.multiply, 5, 2);
```

But we then lose the naturally readable Chai dot-notation syntax.

What we really want is a code that fails with an error message resembling `expected multiply to have been called with arguments 5, 2` and an assertion that reads as follows:

```
expect(obj.multiply).to.be.calledWith(5, 2);
```

Fortunately, we *can* get the best of both the worlds — readable Chai assertions with informative library-specific failure messages — by using Chai's plugin capabilities.

Introducing and installing Chai plugins

Chai supports plugins (`http://chaijs.com/plugins`) that modify and extend the Chai assertion API with contextually useful changes and failure messages. In this section, we will introduce and install the Sinon.JS adapter for Chai, giving us much more concise and ultimately useful assertions for our test doubles.

 The use of the Sinon.JS adapter is recommended but entirely optional. Although we will use the plugin in many examples throughout the rest of the book, all of our test assertions could be rewritten in equivalent statements using native Chai.

The **Sinon-Chai** plugin (`http://chaijs.com/plugins/sinon-chai`) can be downloaded from GitHub at `https://raw.github.com/domenic/sinon-chai/2.4.0/lib/sinon-chai.js`. At present we are using version 2.4.0. The file should be placed in the same directory (`test/js/lib/`) as our other test libraries and included along with the other libraries in the test driver web page:

```
<!-- JavaScript Test Libraries. -->
<script src="js/lib/mocha.js"></script>
<script src="js/lib/chai.js"></script>
<script src="js/lib/sinon-chai.js"></script>
<script src="js/lib/sinon.js"></script>
```

Sinon-Chai must be included *after* Chai and can be included before or after the Sinon.JS library. With this extra include, we are ready to start writing more readable and informative Chai assertions.

Other Chai plugins that may also be useful for Backbone.js application tests include the adapters for Backbone.js (`http://chaijs.com/plugins/chai-backbone`) and jQuery (`http://chaijs.com/plugins/chai-jquery`). The Backbone.js plugin adds assertions for Backbone.js-specific constructs such as `trigger` (for events) and `routes.to` (for routing). The jQuery plugin proxies various jQuery functions into Chai assertions, enabling statements such as `expect($text).to.have.html("<em>Edit your note!</em>")`.

The Sinon.JS plugin

The Sinon-Chai plugin extends Chai with several spy-related assertions, including the following:

- **Call occurrences**: `expect(spy).to.have.been.called`, `expect(spy).to.have.been.calledOnce`, `expect(spy).to.have.been.calledTwice`, and `expect(spy).to.have.been.calledThrice`

- **Call order**: `expect(spy1).to.have.been.calledAfter(spy2)` and `expect(spy1).to.have.been.calledBefore(spy2)`

- **Call arguments**: `expect(spy).to.have.been.calledWithNew`, `expect(spy).to.have.been.calledOn(context)`, `expect(spy).to.have.been.calledWith(arg1, arg2, ...)`, `expect(spy).to.have.been.calledWithExactly(arg1, arg2, ...)`, and `expect(spy).to.have.been.calledWithMatch(arg1, arg2, ...)`

- **Return values**: `expect(spy).to.have.returned(returnVal)`

- **Errors**: `expect(spy).to.have.thrown()`

The plugin also adds a new assertion flag:

- `always`: It signals that the spied function must pass the assertion for *every* function call and not just one or more function call. For example, we can convert any of the following assertions that check *any* function call into ones that check *every* call:

```
expect(spy).to.always.have.been.calledWith(arg1, arg2, ...);
expect(spy).to.have.always.returned(returnVal);
expect(spy).to.have.always.thrown();
```

Now, we can rewrite one of our earlier test examples with Sinon-Chai assertions to read as follows:

```
it("calls spy with chai plugin", sinon.test(function () {
    this.spy(obj, "multiply");
    this.spy(obj, "error");

    expect(obj.multiply(5, 2)).to.equal(10);
    expect(obj.multiply).to.have.been.calledWith(5, 2);
    expect(obj.multiply).to.have.returned(10);

    try { obj.error("Foo"); } catch (e) {}
    expect(obj.error).to.have.thrown("Error");
}));
```

Any spy assertion failures in the previous refactored test will produce informative messages such as `expected multiply to have been called with arguments 5, 2`. Thus, the Sinon-Chai plugin allows us to keep the spy assertions in Chai's chained dot-notation format while also producing helpful failure messages.

Testing Backbone.js components with spies

With our Sinon.JS spies and other utilities ready, we will begin spying on our Backbone.js application. In this section, we will introduce and test two Notes application views — the menu bar view and the single note view.

Working through the examples

Reiterating a point from the previous chapter, we will present the menu bar view and single note view implementations with the code *first* and the tests *second*, to help maintain a narrative structure that properly introduces the Notes application (and to keep things brief). This is not the preferred order for actual test development.

Accordingly, while working through this chapter, we suggest that you put this book down for a moment after reading the described behavior of each component. See if you can design and implement your own tests for the sample application components. After this exercise, you can continue reading and compare your tests with the component test suites in this chapter.

The Notes menu bar view

The Notes menu bar view, `App.Views.NoteNav`, controls the **Edit**, **View**, and **Delete** menu bar buttons for a single note. The following screenshot illustrates the menu bar with an active **View** button.

Single page menu bar view

The `App.Views.NoteNav` view coordinates incoming/outgoing events for the view, edit, and delete menu actions. For example, if the **Edit** button was clicked on in the previous figure, the `App.Views.NoteNav` view would emit the following custom Backbone.js events:

- `nav:update:edit`: This causes the active HTML menu bar item to switch to a new selected action, for example, changing from **View** to **Edit**.

- `nav:edit`: This is emitted to signal other Backbone.js components that the operative action (for example, view or edit) has changed. For example, the `App.Views.Note` view listens on this event and displays HTML for the appropriate corresponding action pane in its view area.

The menu bar view is attached to the DOM list `#note-nav`, which is provided by the `notes/app/index.html` application page. The HTML for `#note-nav` can be abbreviated to the following essential parts:

```
<ul id="note-nav"
  class="nav region region-note"
  style="display: none;">
  <li class="note-view active">View</li>
  <li class="note-edit">Edit</li>
  <li class="note-delete">Delete</li>
</ul>
```

The menu bar list is hidden by default (but shown by `App.Views.Note`). After instantiation, the `App.Views.NoteNav` view sets up various listeners and activates the proper menu bar item.

The menu bar view

Now that we have reviewed the display setup and overall functionality of the view, we can dive into the application code at `notes/app/js/app/views/note-nav.js`:

```
App.Views.NoteNav = Backbone.View.extend({

  el: "#note-nav",
```

After specifying a default `el` element to attach the view to, the view binds the user menu bar clicks to the appropriate actions (for example, edit) in `events` and sets listeners in `initialize` to update the menu bar on occurrence of external events:

```
events: {
  "click .note-view":   "clickView",
  "click .note-edit":   "clickEdit",
  "click .note-delete": "clickDelete",
},

initialize: function () {
  // Defaults for nav.
  this.$("li").removeClass("active");

  // Update the navbar UI for view/edit (not delete).
  this.on({
    "nav:update:view": this.updateView,
    "nav:update:edit": this.updateEdit
  });
},
```

The functions `updateView` and `updateEdit` switch the `active` CSS class, which visually changes the highlighted tab in the menu bar:

```
updateView: function () {
  this.$("li").not(".note-view").removeClass("active");
  this.$(".note-view").addClass("active");
},
updateEdit: function () {
  this.$("li").not(".note-edit").removeClass("active");
  this.$(".note-edit").addClass("active");
},
```

The `clickView`, `clickEdit`, and `clickDelete` functions emit the view events corresponding to the menu bar actions:

```
clickView: function () {
  this.trigger("nav:update:view nav:view");
  return false;
},
clickEdit: function () {
  this.trigger("nav:update:edit nav:edit");
  return false;
},
clickDelete: function () {
  this.trigger("nav:update:delete nav:delete");
  return false;
}
});
```

Testing and spying on the menu bar view

The `App.Views.NoteNav` view is fairly small and essentially just proxies events and updates the menu bar UI. Our testing goals are similarly modest:

- Verify that `App.Views.NoteNav` is bound to the DOM correctly, either by defaulting to `#note-nav` or via a passed `el` parameter
- Check that the menu bar action events are triggered and listened to correctly
- Ensure that the menu bar HTML is modified in response to appropriate actions

With these guidelines in mind, let's step through `chapters/04/test/js/spec/views/note-nav.spec.js`, which is the suite for the menu bar view.

The suite starts out by setting up a test fixture and a view. The `before()` call creates the minimum HTML that we will need to produce a menu bar list suitable for testing the view. The `beforeEach()` function attaches `this.$fixture` to the `#fixtures` container already in the DOM and creates a new `App.Views.NoteNav` object. The `afterEach()` call removes the view and `after()` empties out the `#fixtures` container completely:

```
describe("App.Views.NoteNav", function () {
  before(function () {
    this.$fixture = $(
      "<ul id='note-nav'>" +
        "<li class='note-view'></li>" +
        "<li class='note-edit'></li>" +
        "<li class='note-delete'></li>" +
      "</ul>"
```

```
      );
    });

    beforeEach(function () {
      this.$fixture.appendTo($("#fixtures"));
      this.view = new App.Views.NoteNav({
        el: this.$fixture
      });
    });

    afterEach(function () {
      this.view.remove();
    });

    after(function () {
      $("#fixtures").empty();
    });
```

The first nested suite, `events`, contains one spec that verifies if a click on a menu bar item fires the appropriate `nav:*` and `nav:update:*` events. We create three Sinon.JS spies to help us with this task:

- `navSpy` and `updateSpy`: These objects spy on the events `nav:view` and `nav:update:view` and should be called when the **View** menu bar item is clicked on

- `otherSpy`: This spy listens on all other potential action events and is used to check whether the other events did *not* fire

We use the Sinon-Chai adapter extensions to make our spy assertions:

```
describe("events", function () {
  it("fires events on 'view' click", function () {
    var navSpy = sinon.spy(),
      updateSpy = sinon.spy(),
      otherSpy = sinon.spy();

    this.view.on({
      "nav:view": navSpy,
      "nav:update:view": updateSpy,
      "nav:edit nav:update:edit": otherSpy,
      "nav:delete nav:update:delete": otherSpy
```

```
        });

        this.$fixture.find(".note-view").click();

        expect(navSpy).to.have.been.calledOnce;
        expect(updateSpy).to.have.been.calledOnce;
        expect(otherSpy).to.not.have.been.called;
      });
    });
```

The specs in the `menu bar display` suite inspect DOM content and page interactions with the view. The first spec, `has no active navs by default`, checks that the menu bar HTML has no active selection by default—which, for a Bootstrap-based navigation bar, means the absence of the `active` CSS class:

```
    describe("menu bar display", function () {
      it("has no active navs by default", function () {
        // Check no list items are active.
        expect(this.view.$("li.active")).to.have.length(0);

        // Another way - manually check each list nav.
        expect($(".note-view")
          .attr("class")).to.not.include("active");
        expect($(".note-edit")
          .attr("class")).to.not.include("active");
        expect($(".note-delete")
          .attr("class")).to.not.include("active");
      });
```

Then, the remaining specs check whether clicking on the **Edit** menu bar tab or firing a direct `nav:update:edit` event causes the corresponding menu bar item to be activated (via insertion of the CSS class `active`):

```
      it("updates nav on 'edit' click", function () {
        $(".note-edit").click();
        expect($(".note-edit").attr("class")).to.include("active");
      });

      it("updates nav on 'edit' event", function () {
        this.view.trigger("nav:update:edit");
        expect($(".note-edit").attr("class")).to.include("active");
      });
    });
  });
```

With the previous tests, we can verify that `App.Views.NoteNav` fires appropriate events and its HTML responds to user clicks and external events.

The Notes single note view

The `App.Views.Note` view controls everything that we have encountered so far with respect to a single note. Each `App.Views.Note` object instantiates a new `App.Views.NoteView` object and refers to an external `App.Views.NoteNav` object.

The main responsibilities of the class, which we will want to verify in the tests, include the following:

- Update the appropriate viewing pane mode (for example, edit or view) in response to menu bar action events
- Delete a single note model, and then clean up views and route back to the all notes list view
- Require user confirmation before deleting a note
- Save note model data into the backend storage in response to edit form field changes
- Update the HTML display panes in response to model data changes

We will first look at the HTML template string used by the view. It is found in our application template file, `notes/app/js/app/templates/templates.js`:

```
App.Templates["template-note"] =
  "<div id=\"note-pane-view\" class=\"pane\">" +
  "  <div id=\"note-pane-view-content\"></div>" +
  "</div>" +
  "<div id=\"note-pane-edit\" class=\"pane\">" +
  "  <form id=\"note-form-edit\">" +
  "    <input id=\"input-title\" class=\"input-block-level\"" +
  "           type=\"text\" placeholder=\"title\"" +
  "           value=\"<%= title %>\">" +
  "    <textarea id=\"input-text\" class=\"input-block-level\"" +
  "              rows=\"15\"><%= text %></textarea>" +
  "  </form>" +
  "</div>";
```

The template provides two `div` UI panes for action modes — `note-pane-view` for *viewing* a note and `note-pane-edit` for *editing* data. It also binds two template variables — `title` and `text` — to the editing inputs in the `note-form-edit` form.

The single note view

Getting into the application code at notes/app/js/app/views/note-nav.js, we start by declaring the DOM identifier and template and then set up two events—the first one saves note data on occurrence of the browser's blur event, and the second one prevents the editing form from doing a real HTTP page submission:

```
App.Views.Note = Backbone.View.extend({

  id: "note-panes",

  template: _.template(App.Templates["template-note"]),

  events: {
    "blur   #note-form-edit": "saveNote",
    "submit #note-form-edit": function () { return false; }
  },
```

The initialize function does most of the heavy lifting for the view. First, it sets this.nav from the parameter options and this.router from either options or from the external app application object.

> The reason we optionally take a router object from the opts parameter is that it makes it easier to override Backbone.js dependencies. In our tests, we will use opts to pass a Sinon.JS spy instead of a real router that records behavior but doesn't actually route. A different approach to this scenario (introduced in the next chapter) is to stub or mock app.router directly.

Then, the view sets up event listeners on various objects by calling the helper function _addListeners. Finally, the view object renders its Underscore.js template to HTML with model data, sets the action state, and instantiates a child App.Views.NoteView object to handle Markdown rendering:

```
initialize: function (attrs, opts) {
    opts || (opts = {});
    this.nav = opts.nav;
    this.router = opts.router || app.router;

    // Add our custom listeners.
    this._addListeners();

    // Render HTML, update to action, and show note.
    this.$el.html(this.template(this.model.toJSON()));
    this.update(opts.action || "view");
```

```
      this.render();

      // Add in viewer child view (which auto-renders).
      this.noteView = new App.Views.NoteView({
        el: this.$("#note-pane-view-content"),
        model: this.model
      });
    },
```

As a part of initialization, the _addListeners helper binds object events as follows:

- **Model** (this.model): The view removes itself when the model is destroyed. It re-renders and saves the model to the backend when the model data changes.

- **Menu bar view** (this.nav): The note view listens to the menu bar nav events and calls specific action functions such as viewNote() when a user clicks on **View**.

- **Note view** (this): The note view also directly listens for action state (viewing or editing) events from external Backbone.js components. For instance, the application router uses these events to activate an existing App.Views.Note view object and set an appropriate action state.

Translating this into code produces the following function:

```
  _addListeners: function () {
    // Model controls view rendering and existence.
    this.listenTo(this.model, {
      "destroy": function () { this.remove(); },
      "change":  function () { this.render().model.save(); }
    });

    // Navbar controls/responds to panes.
    this.listenTo(this.nav, {
      "nav:view":   function () { this.viewNote(); },
      "nav:edit":   function () { this.editNote(); },
      "nav:delete": function () { this.deleteNote(); }
    });

    // Respond to update events from router.
    this.on({
      "update:view": function () { this.render().viewNote(); },
      "update:edit": function () { this.render().editNote(); }
    });
  },
```

The `render()` function displays the HTML for the single note view and hides any HTML content used by other views:

```
// Rendering the note is simply showing the active pane.
// All HTML should already be rendered during initialize.
render: function () {
  $(".region").not(".region-note").hide();
  $(".region-note").show();
  return this;
},
```

The `remove()` method first removes the contained `App.Views.NoteView` object and then the `App.Views.Note` object itself:

```
remove: function () {
  // Remove child, then self.
  this.noteView.remove();
  Backbone.View.prototype.remove.call(this);
},
```

The `update()` method takes an action string parameter (`"view"` or `"edit"`), then triggers the menu bar view to update to the new state, shows the appropriate HTML action pane, and updates the URL hash fragment:

```
update: function (action) {
  action = action || this.action || "view";
  var paneEl = "#note-pane-" + action,
    loc = "note/" + this.model.id + "/" + action;

  // Ensure menu bar is updated.
  this.nav.trigger("nav:update:" + action);

  // Show active pane.
  this.$(".pane").not(paneEl).hide();
  this.$(paneEl).show();

  // Store new action and navigate.
  if (this.action !== action) {
    this.action = action;
    this.router.navigate(loc, { replace: true });
  }
},
```

The next three methods—`viewNote()`, `editNote()`, and `deleteNote()`—handle the basic actions for a single note. The first two methods simply call `update()` with the appropriate action, while `deleteNote()` destroys the note model and routes back to the all notes list (that is, the application home page):

```
viewNote: function () {
  this.update("view");
},
editNote: function () {
  this.update("edit");
},
deleteNote: function () {
  if (confirm("Delete note?")) {
    this.model.destroy();
    this.router.navigate("", { trigger: true, replace: true });
  }
},
```

Finally, `saveNote()` takes the edit form input and updates the underlying note model:

```
saveNote: function () {
  this.model.set({
    title: this.$("#input-title").val().trim(),
    text: this.$("#input-text").val().trim()
  });
}
});
```

Testing the single note view

Our tests for `App.Views.Note` center around the various responsibilities of the class we discussed while introducing the view. Specifically, we want to verify that the note view can update UI elements for actions (for example, view and edit), delete notes, save model data, and correctly bind events across various other Backbone.js application components.

Walking through `chapters/04/test/js/spec/views/note.spec.js`, the single note test suite, we start by creating an initial test state. In the suite-wide `before()` function, we add fixture elements for regions (of which `App.Views.Note` uses region-note), an HTML fixture for the view itself, and then stub the note model prototype's `save()` method.

While Sinon.JS stubs are not fully introduced in this chapter, we use one here to record calls to `save()` like a spy and also to prevent the method from trying to save to a remote backend, which would throw an error in this test context.

```
describe("App.Views.Note", function () {

  before(function () {
    // Regions for different views.
    $("#fixtures").append($(
      "<div class='region-note' style='display: none;'></div>" +
      "<div class='region-notes' style='display: none;'></div>"
    ));

    // App.Views.Note fixture.
    this.$fixture = $(
      "<div id='note-fixture region-note'>" +
        "<div id='#note-pane-view-content'></div>" +
      "</div>"
    );

    // Any model changes will trigger a `model.save()`, which
    // won't work in the tests, so we have to fake the method.
    sinon.stub(App.Models.Note.prototype, "save");
  });
```

In the `beforeEach()` setup method, we attach the view fixtures to the fixture container and create a spy function meant to replace our real Backbone.js router. Then, we create an `App.Views.Note` object and bind the fixtures and a new `App.Models.Note` to it. We also provide two initialization options to the `App.Views.Note` instance:

- `nav`: We pass a raw `Backbone.View` object as a replacement for the menu bar view to proxy events through, while omitting the real view logic and DOM interaction

- `router`: We pass `this.routerSpy` to record the Backbone.js routing events without actually changing our browser history/URL state

```
beforeEach(function () {
    this.routerSpy = sinon.spy();
    this.$fixture.appendTo($("#fixtures"));

    this.view = new App.Views.Note({
      el: this.$fixture,
      model: new App.Models.Note()
```

```
  }, {
    nav: new Backbone.View(),
    router: {
      navigate: this.routerSpy
    }
  });
});
```

It is worth noting that we inject four view dependencies (`el`, `model`, `nav`, and `router`) into `App.Views.Note` to help isolate the instance and make it testable. With this configuration, the specs in our suite could be considered partial integration tests because we are using (and testing) real Backbone.js objects beyond the view under test.

Another observation with the previous setup is that the `nav` and `router` option parameters are specifically chosen to avoid triggering the real behavior of the full application; for example, manipulating the menu bar DOM or changing the browser's URL. As we will learn in *Chapter 5, Test Stubs and Mocks*, this type of behavior replacement is much more concisely and appropriately performed with Sinon.JS stubs or mocks.

Moving on to the test teardown in `afterEach()`, we clear out the test fixtures and delete any view objects still around. (The specs may already have destroyed the test view object.) Finally, at the end of the suite in `after()`, we clear out the top-level fixture container and restore the `save()` method of the `App.Models.Note` class to its original state:

```
afterEach(function () {
  this.$fixture.empty();
  if (this.view) { this.view.model.destroy(); }
});

after(function () {
  $("#fixtures").empty();
  App.Models.Note.prototype.save.restore();
});
```

With our setup/teardown complete, we move on to the first nested test suite, `view modes and actions`, which verifies that the user DOM interaction and Backbone.js events can control the note view and cause it to switch between editing, viewing, and deleting modes:

```
describe("view modes and actions", function () {
```

By default, an `App.Views.Note` view routes to the URL hash fragment `#note/:id/view` and displays the viewing mode HTML. We use our router spy to verify the suffix of the called hash fragment using the Sinon-Chai `calledWithMatch` extension. Then, we assert that only the viewing pane `#note-pane-view` is visible with a simple CSS `display` property check:

```
it("navigates / displays 'view' by default", function () {
    expect(this.routerSpy).to.be.calledWithMatch(/view$/);

    // Check CSS visibility directly. Not necessarily a best
    // practice as it uses internal knowledge of the DOM, but
    // gets us a quick check on what should be the visible
    // view pane.
    expect($("#note-pane-view")
      .css("display")).to.not.equal("none");
    expect($("#note-pane-edit")
      .css("display")).to.equal("none");
});
```

The next spec triggers the `update:edit` event and then verifies that this changes the URL hash fragment to `#note/:id/edit` and displays the editing pane:

```
it("navigates / displays 'edit' on event", function () {
    this.view.trigger("update:edit");
    expect(this.routerSpy).to.be.calledWithMatch(/edit$/);

    expect($("#note-pane-edit")
      .css("display")).to.not.equal("none");
    expect($("#note-pane-view")
      .css("display")).to.equal("none");
});
```

We test the note deletion behavior by stubbing out the `confirm()` pop up to always return `false` (preventing the actual note deletion) and then calling `deleteNote()`. We need this stub to prevent an actual browser confirmation window from popping up during our test run. Then, we use the spy properties of the stub to verify that `confirm()` was called correctly:

```
it("confirms note on delete", sinon.test(function () {
    this.stub(window, "confirm").returns(false);
    this.view.deleteNote();
    expect(window.confirm)
      .to.have.been.calledOnce.and
      .to.have.been.calledWith("Delete note?");
}));
});
```

The next test suite, `model interaction`, contains a single spec that verifies that the deletion of a model causes the `App.Views.Note` object to remove itself and its contained `App.Views.NoteView` object. Accordingly, we set up spies on the `remove()` methods of both the views.

Failure to clean up the views, models, and so on once they are no longer used can lead to memory leaks, which may have significant impact on the overall application performance. Triggering `App.Views.Note` and `App.Views.NoteView` object removals on the destruction of the underlying note model is one way of reclaiming used memory from the various components of a Backbone.js application.

At the same time, there are many other techniques to keep the memory in check. *Zombies! RUN!* (`http://lostechies.com/derickbailey/2011/09/15/zombies-run-managing-page-transitions-in-backbone-apps/`) and *Backbone.js And JavaScript Garbage Collection* (`http://lostechies.com/derickbailey/2012/03/19/backbone-js-and-javascript-garbage-collection/`) are posts by *Derick Bailey* that provide a great introduction to Backbone.js memory management issues and solutions.

```
describe("model interaction", function () {
  afterEach(function () {
    // Wipe out to prevent any further use.
    this.view = null;
  });

  it("is removed on destroyed model", sinon.test(function () {
    this.spy(this.view, "remove"),
    this.spy(this.view.noteView, "remove");

    this.view.model.trigger("destroy");

    expect(this.view.remove).to.be.calledOnce;
    expect(this.view.noteView.remove).to.be.calledOnce;
  });
});
```

The last nested test suite, `note rendering`, checks that model data is correctly rendered to HTML and that rendering is triggered in response to expected application events. The first spec, `can render a note`, verifies that `render()` shows the appropriate HTML region elements and hides the rest:

```
describe("note rendering", function () {

  it("can render a note", function () {
```

```
        // Don't explicitly call `render()` because
        // `initialize()` already called it.
        expect($(".region-note")
          .css("display")).to.not.equal("none");
        expect($(".region-notes")
          .css("display")).to.equal("none");
      });
```

The next two specs check that the render() method is triggered on appropriate changes. The spec calls render on model events verifies that render() is called whenever the model changes:

```
      it("calls render on model events", sinon.test(function () {
        // Spy on `render` and check call/return value.
        this.spy(this.view, "render");

        this.view.model.trigger("change");

        expect(this.view.render)
          .to.be.calledOnce.and
          .to.have.returned(this.view);
      }));
```

The final spec modifies data in the single note edit form like a user would and then triggers the blur event to force model change events. The spec spies on the render() method and checks that the rendered Markdown HTML has been updated to reflect the new data:

```
      it("calls render on changed data", sinon.test(function () {
        this.spy(this.view, "render");

        // Replace form value and blur to force changes.
        $("#input-text").val("# A Heading!");
        $("#note-form-edit").blur();

        // `Note` view should have rendered.
        expect(this.view.render)
          .to.be.calledOnce.and
          .to.have.returned(this.view);

        // Check the `NoteView` view rendered the new markdown.
        expect($("#pane-text").html())
          .to.match(/<h1 id=".*?">A Heading!<\/h1>/);
      }));
    });
  });
```

With all of the specs in this suite, we have increased confidence that the App.Views. Note class can emit/listen to appropriate events, clean up application objects on model deletion, and other behaviors that we earlier identified as the core responsibilities of the view.

Hooking up and running the view tests

Now that we have our test suites for App.Views.NoteNav and App.Views.Note, let's wire up the test driver page chapters/04/test/test.html. We can re-use the same code as in chapters/03/test/test.html, with a few (highlighted in the ensuing code) differences, that add in the Sinon-Chai plugin, more Notes application libraries, and our new spec files:

```html
<head>
  <!-- ... snipped ... -->

  <!-- JavaScript Test Libraries. -->
  <script src="js/lib/mocha.js"></script>
  <script src="js/lib/chai.js"></script>
  <script src="js/lib/sinon-chai.js"></script>
  <script src="js/lib/sinon.js"></script>

  <!-- JavaScript Core Libraries -->
  <!-- ... snipped ... -->

  <!-- JavaScript Application Libraries -->
  <script src="../app/js/app/namespace.js"></script>
  <script src="../app/js/app/config.js"></script>
  <script>
    // Test overrides (before any app components).
    App.Config = _.extend(App.Config, {
      storeName: "notes-test" // localStorage for tests.
    });
  </script>
  <script src="../app/js/app/models/note.js"></script>
  <script src="../app/js/app/collections/notes.js"></script>
  <script src="../app/js/app/templates/templates.js"></script>
  <script src="../app/js/app/views/note-nav.js"></script>
  <script src="../app/js/app/views/note-view.js"></script>
  <script src="../app/js/app/views/note.js"></script>

  <!-- ... snipped ... -->

  <!-- Tests. -->
  <script src="js/spec/views/note-nav.spec.js"></script>
  <script src="js/spec/views/note.spec.js"></script>
</head>
```

We can run the tests by opening a browser to `chapters/04/test/test.html`. (Note that the code samples contain the additional specs that are omitted from this chapter for brevity).

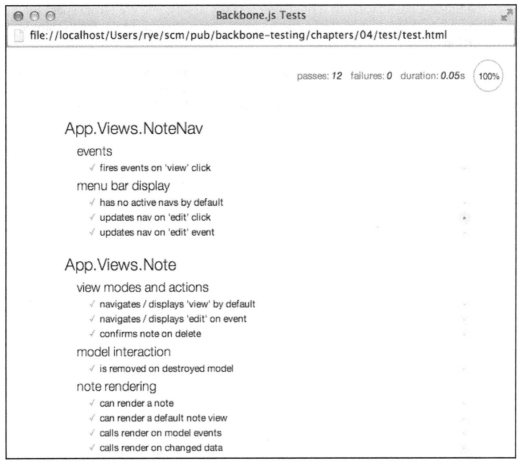

Test report

Summary

We introduced the Sinon.JS test library in this chapter and learned how to integrate spies in various testing scenarios. We investigated Chai's plugin architecture and used the Sinon-Chai adapter to write better test spy assertions. We wrote specs for the menu bar and single note Backbone.js views, completing our tests for the single note portion of the Notes application.

The next chapter continues our exploration of Sinon.JS by looking into stubs, mocks, and other useful fake testing objects. We will use these tools to fill out more parts of our Backbone.js application test collection and round out the fundamentals of writing tests with Mocha, Chai, and Sinon.JS.

5
Test Stubs and Mocks

With the integration of Sinon.JS into our test infrastructure, we now have deeper insight into the methods and actions within our Backbone.js application. As we turn to testing the remaining application components, we will move beyond merely *observing* methods during tests and actually *replace* method behaviors.

Sinon.JS has us covered in this respect as well — the library provides solid support for functional behavior modifications. Specifically, we can leverage its powerful stub and mock abstractions to reduce Backbone.js component dependencies and cross-application side effects during testing. In this chapter, we will explore these and other Sinon.JS capabilities through the following topics:

- Using Sinon.JS stubs to replace function behaviors and isolate Backbone.js components in tests

- Introducing Sinon.JS mocks that spy, stub, and verify application behavior in a single abstraction

- Writing tests for the remaining components of our Backbone.js application and deciding on the proper Sinon.JS tools for the given test scenarios

- Investigating other contextually useful Sinon.JS test helpers

- Faking a remote backend server in Backbone.js collection tests

Replacing method behaviors with Sinon.JS stubs

We have been able to handle our Backbone.js testing dependencies so far with a combination of clever class design and some manual faking. However, we are quickly approaching a point where we need a more reliable and consistent approach.

We will look to stubs to provide a straightforward and predictable means of substituting method behaviors in any Backbone.js component to reduce unintended application side effects and dependency issues. The ability to temporarily replace existing methods during tests offers an enormous amount of flexibility, particularly in situations where:

- A Backbone.js application is under early development and not all of the planned components exist. Stubs allow us to write a simulated equivalent of the missing functionality in tests that can later be removed when the real application code is written. Even after the application code has been implemented, stubs may still be appropriate for a subset of the original specs, depending on what type of behavior is being tested.

- An application code is sensitive to the timing of the UI and/or other events.

- An application depends on external resources such as a database or cloud service.

- A Backbone.js component has application dependencies and/or interactions that are too complex to manually swap in tests and that must be faked internally.

Getting started with stubs

To kick things off, let's integrate some stubs into an object literal from the previous chapter:

```
var obj = {
  multiply: function (a, b) { return a * b; },
  error: function (msg) { throw new Error(msg); }
};
```

In the ensuing spec, we will show you two different ways to stub `obj.multiply()` with Sinon.JS. In the first call (`sinon.stub(obj, "multiply").returns(5)`), we use the `returns` method to always return a hardcoded value. The second stub takes an alternate approach that inserts a replacement function (that adds instead of multiplying). In both cases, we call `restore()` after the test finishes to keep `obj` from being permanently modified:

```
it("stubs multiply", function () {
  // Stub with a hard-coded return value.
  sinon.stub(obj, "multiply").returns(5);
  expect(obj.multiply(1, 2)).to.equal(5);
  obj.multiply.restore();

  // Stub with a function.
  sinon.stub(obj, "multiply", function (a, b) {
    return a + b;
  });
  expect(obj.multiply(1, 2)).to.equal(3);
  obj.multiply.restore();
});
```

Turning our attention to `obj.error()` in the ensuing code snippet, we create an empty stub on the object method to prevent the real function from throwing an exception. We don't need a replacement function or a `returns` value because we just want to *avoid* the default behavior. Additionally, we use the `sinon.test` sandbox helper to automatically call `restore()` on any stubs that were created within the test function:

```
it("stubs error", sinon.test(function () {
  this.stub(obj, "error");
  expect(obj.error).to.not.throw();
}));
```

As illustrated in the previous code snippets, we can now easily replace arbitrary methods with different code and/or return values.

The stub API

Sinon.JS stubs implement the entire spy API and provide additional methods that can swap existing application functions with new code and behaviors during our tests. The first step in stubbing is to create a stub object and potentially replace one or more object methods:

- `sinon.stub()`: This creates an anonymous stub without any specified behavior.

- `sinon.stub(obj, methodName)`: This stubs a single object's method with an empty function. This alone is sufficient to replace the underlying code's execution like we saw in the code with `obj.error()`. Alternatively, you can further call stub API methods to modify return, callback, or other behaviors of the stub.

- `sinon.stub(obj, methodName, fn)`: This stubs a single object's method with the replacement function provided in the `fn` parameter.

- `sinon.stub(obj)`: This replaces *all* the methods in an object with stubs.

Once we have a stub object, we can enhance it with fake behaviors and responses as applicable in a given testing situation. Some of these methods are appropriate for synchronous (non-callback) function responses:

- `stub.returns(obj)`: This stub will return the value `obj` when called.

- `stub.throws()`: This stub will throw an `Error object` exception when called. A specific error will be used if `throws()` is called with a type string (for example, `"TypeError"`) or an error object (for example, `new TypeError()`).

Sinon.JS also supports asynchronous callbacks in stubbed methods:

- `stub.yields(arg1, arg2, ...)`: The first parameter to the stubbed method must be a callback function that the stub will call with the parameters `arg1`, `arg2`, and so on. In the following code snippet, we'll stub `obj.async()` and use `yield()` to inject the fake arguments 1 and 2 into the callback:

```
it("stubs with yields", function (done) {
  var obj = {
    async: function (callback) { callback("a", "b"); }
  };

  sinon.stub(obj, "async").yields(1, 2);

  // Verify stub calls with (1, 2), *not* ("a", "b").
```

```
      obj.async(function (first, second) {
        expect(first).to.equal(1);
        expect(second).to.equal(2);

        obj.async.restore();
        done();
      });
    });
```

- `stub.yieldsOn(context, arg1, arg2, ...)`: This is equivalent to `stub.yields()`, except that it also injects the `context` parameter as the special variable `this` when invoking the callback.

- `stub.yieldsTo(property, arg1, arg2, ...)`: This is also similar to `stub.yields()`, except that the callback to the underlying method is expected to be an object with a property name matching the `property` parameter value.

- `stub.yieldsToOn(property, context, arg1, arg2, ...)`: This is a combination of `stub.yieldsOn()` and `stub.yieldsTo()` that uses an object callback property and context variable.

- `stub.callsArgWith(index, arg1, arg2, ...)`: The `stub.yields*` collection of methods utilizes the *first* parameter of the stubbed method. However, asynchronous callbacks can occur in other parameter positions. The `stub.callsArgWith()` method allows us to specify the index of the callback parameter to be used and the arguments to be passed to the function.

- `stub.callsArg*`: In addition to `stub.callsArgWith()`, the methods `stub.callsArg(index)`, `stub.callsArgOn(index, context)`, and `stub.callsArgOnWith(index, context, arg1, arg2, ...)` take a first parameter named `index` that specifies the index of the callback to be invoked in the wrapped method and work in a manner analogous to their `yields*` counterparts mentioned previously.

This set of stub features is sufficient to cover most Backbone.js testing situations. At the same time, it is worthwhile to review the full Sinon.JS stub API documentation (`http://sinonjs.org/docs/#stubs`) to learn about additional methods and helpers.

Faking and verifying behavior with Sinon.JS mocks

The final test double abstraction that we will cover in this book is the test mock. Mocks replace function behaviors like stubs, observe method calls like spies and stubs, and additionally verify function behaviors. Essentially, mocks are a "one-stop shop" for faking and testing methods.

Deciding when to mock

So, when should we use mocks? The Sinon.JS mock API documentation (`http://sinonjs.org/docs/#mocks`) starts with the appropriate use cases for mocks:

> *"Mocks should only be used for the method under test. In every unit test, there should be one unit under test. If you want to control how your unit is being used and like stating expectations upfront (as opposed to asserting after the fact), use a mock."*

The documentation cautions that mocks should be *avoided* in many situations:

> *"Mocks come with built-in expectations that may fail your test. Thus, they enforce implementation details. The rule of thumb is: if you wouldn't add an assertion for some call specific, don't mock it. Use a stub instead. In general you should never have more than one mock (possibly with several expectations) in a single test."*

We have a bias in this book towards Sinon.JS stubs for the reasons just discussed and because of the following:

- The Chai and Sinon-Chai adapter libraries allow us to write test assertions on stubs that are concise, expressive, and readable
- The Sinon.JS mock expectation API is less flexible than using Chai assertions against the stub API

At the same time, mocks *are* stubs. So, tests can mix and match preprogrammed Sinon.JS mock expectations with subsequent Chai stub assertions. Ultimately, after we have finished reviewing the details of stubs and mocks in this chapter, we leave the choice of abstraction up to the developer and the specific testing scenario at hand.

The mock API

Sinon.JS mocks (`http://sinonjs.org/docs/#mocks-api`) implement the spy and stub APIs and additionally provide expectations that verify application behavior. We'll begin with a brief discussion of the core mock methods:

- `sinon.mock(obj)`: This method mocks all the methods of `obj` and returns a mock object

- `mock.expects(methodName)`: This method creates an expectation for the specified method of the mocked object

- `mock.verify()`: This method examines and verifies that all expectations were met and throws exceptions on assertion failures

- `mock.restore()`: This method unwinds and removes all mocked modifications of the underlying object that is being tested

After we have mocked an object, the usual workflow is to call `mock.expects()` on one or more methods and configure expectations for a `mock.verify()` call later. For the complete expectations list, see `http://sinonjs.org/docs/#expectations`. A sampling of some useful expectation methods includes the following:

- `expectation.atLeast(num)`, `expectation.atMost(num)`, and `expectation.exactly(num)`: These mocked methods should be called at least/at most/exactly `num` times respectively

- `expectation.never()`, `expectation.once()`, `expectation.twice()`, and `expectation.thrice()`: These are the helpers specifying common assertions for the number of times the mocked method was called

- `expectation.withArgs(arg1, arg2, ...)` and `expectation.withExactArgs(arg1, arg2, ...)`: Every call to the mocked method has at least/exactly the parameters specified in the expectation respectively

- `expectation.on(obj)`: This mocked method should be called with `obj` as the context (`this`) variable

- `expectation.verify()`: This method runs assertions on a specific expectation (as opposed to `mock.verify()` that confirms *all* expectations)

In the following code snippet, we create our `mock` object around `obj` and declare the expectation that `multiply` will be called two to four times and that the first argument to every call will be 2. We then call `multiply` three times with the appropriate parameters. Finally, a single `mock.verify()` call checks if all of the mock expectations were met:

```
// Our (now very familiar) object under test.
var obj = {
  multiply: function (a, b) { return a * b; },
  error: function (msg) { throw new Error(msg); }
};

it("mocks multiply", function () {
  // Create the mock.
  var mock = sinon.mock(obj);

  // The multiply method is expected to be called:
  mock.expects("multiply")
    .atLeast(2)     // 2+ times,
    .atMost(4)      // no more than 4 times, and
    .withArgs(2);   // 2 was first arg on *all* calls.

  // Make 3 calls to `multiply()`.
  obj.multiply(2, 1);
  obj.multiply(2, 2);
  obj.multiply(2, 3);

  // Verify **all** of the previous expectations.
  mock.verify();

  // Restore the object.
  mock.restore();
});
```

Testing Backbone.js components with stubs and mocks

With the addition of stubs and mocks to our test infrastructure, we are ready to tackle the remaining components of our Backbone.js application that we will cover in this book: the `App.Views.NotesItem` view and the `App.Routers.Router` router. For those following along in the code examples, we will integrate the specs for these application components into the test driver page `chapters/05/test/test.html`.

Ensuring stubs and mocks are actually bound

One preliminary Sinon.JS issue that can trip up developers is making sure that spies, stubs, and mocks are actually bound to the expected methods of a Backbone.js application object during a test.

Let's start with a simple Backbone.js view named `MyView`. The view has a custom method named `foo()` that is bound to two event listeners, `wrapped` and `unwrapped`. The listeners are functionally equivalent, except that `wrapped` wraps the call in a function (`function () { this.foo(); }`) while `unwrapped` binds the real (or "naked") `this.foo` method:

```
var MyView = Backbone.View.extend({

  initialize: function () {
    this.on("wrapped", function () { this.foo(); });
    this.on("unwrapped", this.foo);
  },

  foo: function () {
    return "I'm real";
  }

});
```

Although quite similar, the event listeners have an important difference when using Sinon.JS fakes; once `initialize()` is called, naked method references, such as the one passed to `unwrapped`, cannot be faked by Sinon.JS later. The underlying reason is that Sinon.JS can only change properties on the view object and not on the direct method references.

Let's examine a test that instantiates a `MyView` object and then stubs `foo`. When we trigger the `wrapped` listener, our stub is called and returns the faked value `I'm fake`. However, triggering the `unwrapped` listener never calls the stub and invokes the *real* `foo` method instead. Note that we use the Sinon.JS `reset()` method to clear out any recorded function call information and return a spy, stub, or mock to its original state:

```
it("stubs after initialization", sinon.test(function () {
  var myView = new MyView();

  // Stub prototype **after** initialization.
  // Equivalent to:
  // this.stub(myView, "foo").returns("I'm fake");
  this.stub(MyView.prototype, "foo").returns("I'm fake");

  // The wrapped version calls the **stub**.
  myView.foo.reset();
  myView.trigger("wrapped");
  expect(myView.foo)
    .to.be.calledOnce.and
    .to.have.returned("I'm fake");

  // However, the unwrapped version calls the **real** function.
  myView.foo.reset();
  myView.trigger("unwrapped");
  expect(myView.foo).to.not.be.called;
}));
```

One solution to the issue is to stub *before* the object is instantiated. In the following code snippet, creating the stub *before* the call to `new MyView()` correctly hooks the stub into both the `wrapped` and `unwrapped` listeners:

```
it("stubs before initialization", sinon.test(function () {
  // Stub prototype **before** initialization.
  this.stub(MyView.prototype, "foo").returns("I'm fake");

  var myView = new MyView();

  // Now, both versions are correctly stubbed.
  myView.foo.reset();
  myView.trigger("wrapped");
  expect(myView.foo)
    .to.be.calledOnce.and
```

```
      .to.have.returned("I'm fake");

   myView.foo.reset();
   myView.trigger("unwrapped");
   expect(myView.foo)
     .to.be.calledOnce.and
     .to.have.returned("I'm fake");
 }));
```

It is fairly straightforward to keep track of the order in which Backbone.js objects are initialized and stubbed for a single test, such as in the previous two code snippets. However, it is important to keep binding in mind for a test suite setup and teardown, especially when an object is instantiated in a different place from where it will later be mocked or stubbed. Additionally, the issue can manifest in various other places in Backbone.js applications, such as in the following:

- **View events**: Views can declare an `events` property that binds UI events to methods by the string name of the method. This internally behaves similar to a naked function reference when a new view object is initialized by Backbone.js. An example of this type of declaration is as follows:

```
events: {
  "click #id": "foo"
}
```

- **Router routes**: Similarly, routers typically declare a `routes` property that binds hash/URL fragments to named methods on the router object.

The most important takeaway point is to always consider how a Sinon.JS fake will be bound to the Backbone.js component that is being tested. It is sometimes easier to avoid naked function references in a Backbone.js application component, and at other times, it is better to reformulate test code so that stubs can be bound before the component is initialized. In the Notes application, we will use both of the approaches for the remaining tests in this chapter.

The Notes list item view

The last Notes view that we will discuss and test in this book is the list item view. When a user navigates to the home page of the Notes application, they are presented with a list of notes identified by their titles. The `App.Views.NotesItem` view is responsible for rendering each individual note row and allowing a user to view, edit, or delete a note. The following screenshot illustrates the rendered output for a single list item view:

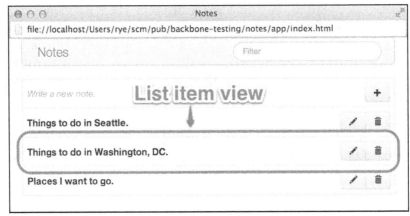

Notes list item view

The title text of a list item can be clicked on to view the rendered Markdown for a single note. A list item also contains two action buttons, one with a pencil icon for editing and the other with a trash can icon for deleting.

The list item template string is declared as the `template-notes-item` property of `App.Templates` in `notes/app/js/app/templates/templates.js`:

```
App.Templates["template-notes-item"] =
  "<td class=\"note-name\">" +
  "  <div class=\"note-title note-view\"><%= title %></div>" +
  "</td>" +
  "<td class=\"note-action\">" +
  "  <div class=\"btn-group pull-right\">" +
  "    <button class=\"btn note-edit\">" +
  "      <i class=\"icon-pencil\"></i>" +
  "    </button>" +
  "    <button class=\"btn note-delete\">" +
  "      <i class=\"icon-trash\"></i>" +
  "    </button>" +
  "  </div>" +
  "</td>";
```

The template renders two `td` cells within a table row, one for the note title and the other for the edit/delete buttons.

The list item view

The `App.Views.NotesItem` view is defined in `notes/app/js/app/views/notes-list.js`. The class definition starts with DOM attributes for rendering a `tr` tag, a `notes-item` class, and an `id` property that corresponds to the note model's identifier:

```
App.Views.NotesItem = Backbone.View.extend({

    id: function () { return this.model.id; },

    tagName: "tr",

    className: "notes-item",

    template: _.template(App.Templates["template-notes-item"]),
```

Click events on a list item's title and edit/delete buttons are bound to their respective view methods, `viewNote`, `editNote`, and `deleteNote`. In terms of our earlier Sinon.JS binding discussion, note that all of the event callbacks have function wrappers that allow us to create `App.Views.NotesItem` objects that can be stubbed at any time during the tests:

```
events: {
  "click .note-view":   function () { this.viewNote(); },
  "click .note-edit":   function () { this.editNote(); },
  "click .note-delete": function () { this.deleteNote(); }
},
```

In `initialize`, the view stores a router reference and sets listeners that re-render or remove the view in response to model events. The `render` method binds the model data to the template in a fairly conventional manner:

```
initialize: function (attrs, opts) {
  opts || (opts = {});
  this.router = opts.router || app.router;

  this.listenTo(this.model, {
    "change":   function () { this.render(); },
    "destroy":  function () { this.remove(); }
  });
},

render: function () {
```

```
      this.$el.html(this.template(this.model.toJSON()));
      return this;
   },
```

Turning to the actions we can perform on a single list item, the `viewNote` and `editNote` methods navigate to a single-note view in viewing or editing mode. The `deleteNote` function deletes the underlying note model that then triggers events that will clean up and remove the view from the list of all notes:

```
viewNote: function () {
   var loc = ["note", this.model.id, "view"].join("/");
   this.router.navigate(loc, { trigger: true });
},

editNote: function () {
   var loc = ["note", this.model.id, "edit"].join("/");
   this.router.navigate(loc, { trigger: true });
},

deleteNote: function () {
   // Destroying model triggers view cleanup.
   this.model.destroy();
}
});
```

Testing the list item view

The `App.Views.NotesItem` view behaviors that we wish to verify in our test suite file `chapters/05/test/js/spec/views/notes-item.spec.js` include the following:

- The view renders HTML for a single row in the notes list table and shows the note's title and the action buttons
- It binds click events to the appropriate note actions (for example, edit) and navigates to the appropriate single note page to read or edit a note
- It correctly cleans up the object state when a user deletes a note

The test suite starts with the `before()` setup method where we create an `App.Views.NotesItem` object with a fake router object literal (containing a `navigate` stub) and a real `App.Models.Note` model. In the `afterEach()` method, we reset the `navigate` stub so that each spec gets a stub that is free of any previously recorded function information. The `after()` teardown function removes the view under test.

Again, keeping the Sinon.JS method's binding issues in mind, we note that `this.`
`view` is created in the `before()` setup for the entire test suite. This means that
stubs, spies, and/or mocks will only work on wrapped `App.Views.NotesItem`
view methods. At the same time, if the existing `App.Views.NotesItem` suite is
not amenable to all of the test double bindings that we need, we can easily create
an additional suite that fakes the class prototype before instantiation, to provide
additional flexibility in testing the desired application behavior:

```
describe("App.Views.NotesItem", function () {

  before(function () {
    this.navigate = sinon.stub();
    this.view = new App.Views.NotesItem({
      model: new App.Models.Note({ id: "0", title: "title" })
    }, {
      router: { navigate: this.navigate }
    });
  });

  afterEach(function () {
    this.navigate.reset();
  });

  after(function () {
    this.view.remove();
  });
```

The first nested test suite checks whether the underlying model's `destroy` event
triggers the `view.remove()` method, cleaning up the view. We stub `view.remove()`
to prevent the view from actually being removed from the test environment when
called. Then, we trigger the desired model event so that we can verify that the stub
was called once:

```
describe("remove", function () {
  it("is removed on model destroy", sinon.test(function () {
    // Empty stub for view removal to prevent side effects.
    this.stub(this.view, "remove");
    this.view.model.trigger("destroy");
    expect(this.view.remove).to.be.calledOnce;
  }));
});
```

In the next two specs, we tackle an analogous scenario, verifying that the note model's change event will trigger a `render()` call on the view. We make the same assertions in both the specs, using stubs in one and mocks in the other to demonstrate how to write the same functional spec using either abstraction. The spec `renders on model change w/ stub` uses a stub to verify the view's behavior:

```
describe("render", function () {
  // One way to verify is with a stub.
  it("renders on model change w/ stub", sinon.test(function () {
    this.stub(this.view);
    this.view.model.trigger("change");
    expect(this.view.render).to.have.been.calledOnce;
  }));
```

In the `renders on model change w/ mock` spec, we rely on a mock to make the same assertion using the Sinon.JS `once()` expectation modifier and `mock.verify()` instead of Chai assertions on a stub:

```
  // Here is another way to do the same check with a mock.
  it("renders on model change w/ mock", sinon.test(function () {
    var exp = this.mock(this.view).expects("render").once();
    this.view.model.trigger("change");
    exp.verify();
  }));
});
```

In the next two specs, we examine the scenarios in which a user clicks on the list item title (for viewing) or the pencil button (for editing). We need to check if both the clicks call an appropriate view function and cause the router to navigate us to the expected single-note page. In the ensuing code snippet, we verify this behavior by asserting that the router's `navigate` stub has been called with appropriate arguments:

```
describe("actions", function () {
  it("views on click", function () {
    this.view.$(".note-view").click();

    expect(this.navigate)
      .to.be.calledOnce.and
      .to.be.calledWith("note/0/view");
  });

  it("edits on click", function () {
    this.view.$(".note-edit").click();

    expect(this.navigate)
      .to.be.calledOnce.and
      .to.be.calledWith("note/0/edit");
  });
```

Finally, we ensure that clicking on the trash can button triggers the underlying note model to be destroyed. We stub the model's `destroy` method to verify that it was called and to prevent the model from actually being mutated:

```
it("deletes on click", sinon.test(function () {
  // Empty stub for model destroy to prevent side effects.
  this.stub(this.view.model, "destroy");
  this.view.$(".note-delete").click();

  expect(this.view.model.destroy).to.be.calledOnce;
}));
  });
});
```

All in all, our tests for `App.Views.NotesItem` demonstrate how replacing method behaviors with mocks and stubs can simplify our tests and limit the program method's side effects.

The Notes application router

The final Backbone.js component that we will test in the Notes application is the router, `App.Routers.Router`. The router is responsible for managing client-side page locations (URLs or hash fragments) and binding routes to views, events, and actions.

For the purposes of this chapter, we will use a simplified version of the `App.Routers.Router` class, available at `chapters/05/test/js/spec/routers/router.js`, instead of the real Notes router file (found in the code samples at `notes/app/js/app/routers/router.js`).

> While the real Backbone.js router is not the most complex beast, it has sufficiently complicated dependencies and application logic to warrant omitting the full implementation in the text of this chapter, particularly when we just need to introduce a few testing tips for routers.
>
> At the same time, we don't shy away from tests just because we have component dependencies. Accordingly, we provide a comprehensive test suite for the real `App.Routers.Router` component in the code samples at `notes/test/js/spec/routers/router.spec.js`. You are encouraged to review the implementations of the full router and its corresponding test suite.

The Notes application contains two routes corresponding to the notes list page and the single-note page. We encompass this behavior in the simplified App.Routers. Router class:

```
App.Routers.Router = Backbone.Router.extend({

  routes: {
    "": "notes",
    "note/:id/:action": "note",
  },

  // Show notes list.
  notes: function () {
    // ... omitted ...
  },

  // Common single note edit/view.
  note: function (noteId, action) {
    // ... omitted ...
  }

});
```

Our tests should check if the route specifications bind to the correct router methods and if the URLs / hash fragments are correctly parsed into parameters for the router method. We verify this behavior in the test suite file chapters/05/test/js/spec/routers/router.spec.js.

Our setup logic begins by creating stubs around the router's note and notes methods. We then instantiate a router object and start history (which enables actual routing). Our setup concludes with binding an anonymous spy to every route event (fired any time a route is activated).

 Always on the lookout for Sinon.JS binding issues, note that we have to stub the router prototype *before* we instantiate a router object because the router object's routes property binds routes to method name strings and not to wrapped functions.

```
describe("App.Routers.Router", function () {

  // Default option: Trigger and replace history.
  var opts = { trigger: true, replace: true };

  beforeEach(function () {
```

```
// Stub route methods.
sinon.stub(App.Routers.Router.prototype, "note");
sinon.stub(App.Routers.Router.prototype, "notes");

// Create router with stubs and manual fakes.
this.router = new App.Routers.Router();

// Start history to enable routes to fire.
Backbone.history.start();

// Spy on all route events.
this.routerSpy = sinon.spy();
this.router.on("route", this.routerSpy);
});
```

Our teardown logic stops the history and unwinds the stubs:

```
afterEach(function () {
  Backbone.history.stop();

  App.Routers.Router.prototype.note.restore();
  App.Routers.Router.prototype.notes.restore();
});
```

The first spec checks if we can navigate to a single note to edit it by calling the router's `navigate` method on the desired route `"note/1/edit"`. We assert that this calls the router's `note` method (which we have stubbed) with the extracted parameters `"1"` and `"edit"`. We also confirm the same type of information with the `routerSpy` event listener:

```
it("can route to note", function () {
  this.router.navigate("note/1/edit", opts);

  // Check router method.
  expect(App.Routers.Router.prototype.note)
    .to.have.been.calledOnce.and
    .to.have.been.calledWithExactly("1", "edit");

  // Check route event.
  expect(this.routerSpy)
    .to.have.been.calledOnce.and
    .to.have.been.calledWith("note", ["1", "edit"]);
});
```

Our second spec verifies that we can navigate to the home page, then to a single-note page, and then back to the home page. We use similar verification logic as in the previous spec, relying on the `notes` stub (called twice on the `""` home page route) and the `routerSpy` spy (called on all three routes):

```
it("can route around", function () {
  // Bounce between routes.
  this.router.navigate("", opts);
  this.router.navigate("note/1/edit", opts);
  this.router.navigate("", opts);

  // Check router method.
  expect(App.Routers.Router.prototype.notes)
    .to.have.been.calledTwice.and
    .to.have.been.calledWithExactly();

  // Check route event.
  expect(this.routerSpy)
    .to.have.been.calledThrice.and
    .to.have.been.calledWith("notes");
});

});
```

These router tests are not that different from Backbone.js view tests for events — both of them bind strings (a route or a UI event) to component methods (via a string name or function). All in all, the Sinon.JS mocking and stubbing methods we have learned in this chapter should generally apply to any type of Backbone.js component.

Running the view and router tests

Now that we have test suites for `App.Views.NotesItem` and `App.Routers.Router`, we can integrate them into a test driver page. Building on the previous `chapters/04/test/test.html` driver page (with a few highlighted additions), our final driver page `chapters/05/test/test.html` includes the following relevant parts:

```
<head>
  <!-- ... snipped ... -->

  <!-- JavaScript Application Libraries -->
  <script src="../app/js/app/namespace.js"></script>
  <script src="../app/js/app/config.js"></script>
  <script>
    // Test overrides (before any app components).
```

```
    App.Config = _.extend(App.Config, {
      storeName: "notes-test" // localStorage for tests.
    });
  </script>
  <script src="../app/js/app/models/note.js"></script>
  <script src="../app/js/app/collections/notes.js"></script>
  <script src="../app/js/app/templates/templates.js"></script>
  <script src="../app/js/app/views/note-nav.js"></script>
  <script src="../app/js/app/views/note-view.js"></script>
  <script src="../app/js/app/views/note.js"></script>
  <script src="../app/js/app/views/notes-item.js"></script>

  <!-- The shortened, teaching router for Chapter 05 -->
  <script src="js/spec/routers/router.js"></script>

  <!-- ... snipped ... -->

  <!-- Tests. -->
  <script src="js/spec/views/notes-item.spec.js"></script>
  <script src="js/spec/routers/router.spec.js"></script>
</head>
```

 At this point, we have accrued a large number of JavaScript files between the vendor libraries and our Backbone.js application components. While this is acceptable for tests (and sometimes even desired), it is good practice to concatenate and optimize your JavaScript files in production applications with a tool such as the Google Closure Compiler (https://developers.google.com/closure/compiler/) or UglifyJS (https://github.com/mishoo/UglifyJS2).

We can now navigate a browser window to `chapters/05/test/test.html` to run the tests.

 If you are running the report from the code samples, a few extra view specs that have not been discussed in this book will appear in the results.

One thing you may notice is that invocations of the `navigate` method in the router tests actually modify the browser location, adding hash fragments. While this doesn't affect the correctness of our tests, it is a bit unexpected. Taking an alternative approach, the Backbone.js library test suite gets around this issue by creating a fake `Location` object to substitute for the real browser navigation bar. See https://github.com/documentcloud/backbone/blob/master/test/router.js for further details.

Finding the rest of the Notes application components

With the previous view and router tests completed, we are now finished with the application and test code that we will present in this book for the localStorage-based Notes application. There are, however, a few more parts of the Notes application that we simply do not have room to discuss within the confines of this book.

Fortunately, each of the components (as well as their relevant test files) are available as part of the downloadable code samples for this book. The remaining parts of the Notes application that you can find in the samples are as follows:

- `App.Views.NotesFilter` (notes/app/js/app/views/notes-filter.js): This view controls the filter input box and the visibility of the note rows in the displayed list of notes. The test file for this view can be found at notes/ test/js/spec/views/notes-filter.spec.js.

- `App.Views.Notes` (notes/app/js/app/views/notes.js): The `App. Views.Notes` view contains the `App.Views.NotesItem` and `App.Views. NotesFilter` views and is responsible for getting note data from the collection and for rendering a full list of notes. The corresponding test file is located at notes/test/js/spec/views/notes.spec.js.

- `App.Routers.Router` (notes/app/js/app/routers/router.js): This is the full implementation of the Backbone.js router for Notes. Its test file is available at notes/test/js/spec/routers/router.spec.js.

- app (notes/app/js/app/app.js): The app object controls the overall Notes application. It instantiates all of the top-level application components; for example, the `App.Views.Notes` view, the `App.Routers.Router` router, and the `App.Collections.Notes` collection. It also kicks off an initial collection `fetch` to import existing notes data. We do not include specs for this file, as creating and starting an actual application is usually encompassed within the scope of full integration testing—an approach we mentioned in *Chapter 2, Creating a Backbone.js Application Test Plan*, which you are encouraged to learn outside of this book.

- notes/test/test.html: This is the test driver page for all the Notes application test suites and specs. This page aggregates all of the Notes specs we have discussed in this book as well as the specs for omitted views, and the full router implementation.

These extra files apply the fundamental lessons we have learned throughout this book to different application code and scenarios. Thus, reviewing the remaining Notes application files will provide you with a much better picture of a full Backbone.js application and test infrastructure that follows the testing principles we suggest. All in all, we hope that the code samples will send home the topics we have covered in this book and possibly give you some ideas and next steps for your test development education.

A few more Sinon.JS test helpers

Sinon.JS provides many useful tools beyond the core test double abstractions of spies, stubs, and mocks. We have already been introduced to the `sinon.test` wrapper in *Chapter 4*, *Test Spies*, and will examine a few more equally convenient helpers in this chapter.

 Some test helpers such as timers and servers may require the use of IE-specific Sinon.JS libraries when used with the Internet Explorer web browser. See the relevant Sinon.JS documentation sections for more details.

Fake timers

Sinon.JS can patch time and date intervals to help manage asynchronous events and callbacks in tests. Sinon.JS fake timers override native JavaScript functions, such as `setTimeout` and the `Date` class. Once faked, test code must manually advance the time through the API `tick(ms)` function that simulates the passage of time for any time-based asynchronous event in the program. See `http://sinonjs.org/docs/#clock` for the full API reference.

Fake timers are quite useful for testing Backbone.js applications. For example, if some UI code has a delayed jQuery effect that is taking 200 milliseconds to complete, a test including this behavior would have to wait for that amount of time, slowing down the overall test suite. Additionally, timers in native JavaScript are not completely predictable. (See, for example, *Accuracy of JavaScript Time* by *John Resig* at `http://ejohn.org/blog/accuracy-of-javascript-time`.) Using Sinon.JS fake timers, we can *synchronously* and *predictably* simulate the advancement of 200 milliseconds for the jQuery effect without any delays in a test.

Fake servers

Sinon.JS can also patch some of the communication internals of a program and override the **XMLHttpRequest (XHR)** and other related mechanisms. A typical Backbone.js application uses XHR to synchronize models and collections to a backend datastore, such as a database or a cloud service, making this feature particularly relevant to our test infrastructure. The entire range of XHR faking capabilities provided by Sinon.JS are discussed at `http://sinonjs.org/docs/#server`.

The fake server API

The first API that Sinon.JS provides is `FakeXMLHttpRequest`; this is a low-level abstraction around the XHR interface that provides fine-grained control over requests, responses, headers, and other details. See `http://sinonjs.org/docs/#FakeXMLHttpRequest` for a complete API listing.

Sinon.JS additionally provides a higher-level API in the form of a fake server that provides a much easier interface for common use cases in modern JavaScript web applications. We will use the latter interface in this chapter as the simpler interface is still well suited to our Backbone.js application testing needs.

The Sinon.JS fake server API documentation is available at `http://sinonjs.org/docs/#fakeServer`. A useful subset of the API includes the following:

- `sinon.fakeServer.create()`: This creates a fake server object and fakes the XHR interface for tests.

- `server.respondWith(response)`: This configures the server to respond to all requests with a response object. A response can take various forms, but the one we will use is an array comprised of an HTTP status code, a dictionary of headers, and a JSON response string. The default response is `[404, {}, ""]`.

- `server.respondWith(method, url, response)`: This configures the server to respond to requests matching the specified HTTP method and URL with a response object. There are further permutations of `respondWith` that can use regular expressions for URL matching.

- `server.respond()`: After a server is configured and a test has started, any call to `respond()` will cause the fake server to immediately issue the prearranged response object.

- `server.autoRespond = true`: The fake server will automatically respond to server requests without the need to call `respond()`. By default, the fake server will wait 10 milliseconds before responding. A different wait time can be assigned to the `server.autoRespondAfter` configuration variable.

- `server.restore()`: This unwinds the fake XHR interface.

Faking the remote backend in a Backbone.js application

The Notes application that we have presented in this book does not have an external backend and relies instead on HTML5 localStorage to store collection data. While it is a useful teaching tool, most real-world Backbone.js applications do have a remote backing store. Accordingly, the companion code examples for this book include a version of Notes that is served as a Node.js Express (`http://expressjs.com`) application with a MongoDB (`http://www.mongodb.org`) backend database. You can find the full application and its test suite in the `notes-rest/` directory of the code examples repository.

The main difference between the localStorage-backed `notes/app` and MongoDB-backed `notes-rest/app` Backbone.js applications is in the `App.Collections.Notes` collection implementation. The `notes-rest/app` version, available at `notes-rest/app/js/app-rest/collections/notes.js`, defines the collection class as follows:

```
App.Collections.Notes = Backbone.Collection.extend({

  model: App.Models.Note,

  url: "/api/notes"

});
```

The URL `/api/notes` points to a backend REST interface provided by the Node.js Express server (`notes-rest/server.js` in the code examples) that interacts with the MongoDB datastore.

Our tests for the new `App.Collections.Notes` collection will rely on a fake server to intercept all of the remote backend calls and replace the network responses with our desired test data.

The collection tests in this section fake the entire backend, meaning that the tests don't use Node.js or MongoDB servers at all. This provides the advantage of the tests running extremely fast and giving us predictable responses. However, testing scenarios that seek to exercise the entire application (for example, full integration tests) may require that the test infrastructure run live on backend servers and/or datastores.

Looking at the test suite file `notes-rest/test/js/spec-rest/collections/` `notes.spec.js` in the `beforeEach` setup call, we create an empty collection and a fake server that automatically responds to backend requests. The `afterEach` call restores the normal XHR operation:

```
describe("App.Collections.Notes", function () {

  beforeEach(function () {
    this.server = sinon.fakeServer.create();
    this.server.autoRespond = true;
    this.notes = new App.Collections.Notes();
  });

  afterEach(function () {
    this.server.restore();
  });
```

The following spec checks if the collection can fetch and populate data from the backend. We configure the fake server to respond to GET requests with JSON-serialized data for a single note. We then set a callback on the `reset` event to verify that the collection has the expected length and has deserialized the data into a note model:

```
describe("retrieval", function () {

  it("has a single note", function (done) {
    var notes = this.notes, note;

    // Return a single model on GET.
    this.server.respondWith("GET", "/api/notes", [
```

```
            200,
            { "Content-Type": "application/json" },
            JSON.stringify([{
              id: 1,
              title: "Test note #1",
              text: "A pre-existing note from beforeEach."
            }])

    ]);

    // After fetch.
    notes.once("reset", function () {
      expect(notes).to.have.length(1);

      // Check model attributes.
      note = notes.at(0);
      expect(note).to.be.ok;
      expect(note.get("title")).to.contain("#1");
      expect(note.get("text")).to.contain("pre-existing");

      done();
    });

    notes.fetch({ reset: true });
  });

});
```

This spec illustrates the simple manner in which requests can be faked—we just make one `this.server.respondWith()` setup call for the specific faked URL and the Backbone.js collection is none the wiser that it is not really talking to a remote data store. For additional collection tests with Sinon.JS fake servers, see the rest of the `notes-rest/test/js/spec-rest/collections/notes.spec.js` file in the companion code samples for this book that can be run from the test driver page `notes-rest/test/test.html`.

Summary

In this chapter, we learned how to apply Sinon.JS stubs, mocks, and other fakes to isolate Backbone.js components, reduce test complexity, and enhance predictable test behavior. We also finished all of the application tests that we will discuss in this book for the reference Notes application. Taking a moment to reflect upon our progress leading up to this point, we have now covered the basics of creating a test infrastructure and applying fundamental testing concepts to all of the various Backbone.js application components.

But, this is really just the beginning of the substantive testing journey; the tests presented in this book are a subset of those that would be desirable for a full production Backbone.js application. Our hope is that you now have the necessary tools, development techniques, and starting points to provide full test support for your Backbone.js applications.

In the next chapter, we will aim at extending our testing capabilities and use cases through test automation. We will move beyond manually running test suites in a local browser and introduce testing tools that can execute tests in different environments (such as the command line or a build server) and without a web browser.

Automated Web Testing

6

Having finished discussing the substantive techniques for testing Backbone.js applications, we will now look into various means of automating our test infrastructure. The ability to programmatically run our test collection enables new and exciting use cases beyond a single developer manually running a test driver page during development. In this chapter we will explore the following automation and development topics:

- Surveying scenarios and motivations for automating our test infrastructure

- Investigating different approaches for programmatically running a Backbone.js application test suite

- Introducing PhantomJS and adapter tools for frontend testing

- Integrating our existing test infrastructure into the PhantomJS environment

- Concluding our discussion on the principles and practices of Backbone.js application testing with suggestions and resources for the next steps after finishing this book

The world of testing beyond humans and browsers

Up to this point, our test development workflow has comprised writing test suites, adding them to a test driver page, and firing up the test page in a web browser on a development computer. However, test infrastructures can be used in far more scenarios than just manually running web reports. Examining the ensuing use cases, we will see how automatically running our test collection in arbitrary environments (for example, from a command line or build script, and possibly without a web browser) has enormous potential for the application development process.

Continuous integration

In collaborative software development, problems can arise when engineers develop code separately that they later merge into a common code base. Unforeseen interactions between the changes can cause integration errors, breaking the overall application.

One mitigation approach for such errors is continuous integration, which relies extensively on automated testing. Continuous integration aggregates and tests application code to detect integration errors early and automatically. For an in-depth introduction on the topic, see *Continuous Integration* by *Martin Fowler* at `http://martinfowler.com/articles/continuousIntegration.html`.

The process of continuous integration is typically implemented using a dedicated server that incrementally gathers code changes, creates a clean application environment, runs build commands, and acts on the command outputs. For instance, let's say we have a Node.js application stored on GitHub. A continuous integration server could download code changes from GitHub, create a new build directory for the application, install package dependencies (for example, `npm install`), and run the tests (for example, `npm test`). If any of the tests fail, the server will notify the developer(s) responsible for the changes. Some prevalent continuous integration servers include Jenkins (`http://jenkins-ci.org/`) and Travis (`https://travis-ci.org/`).

Continuous deployment

A continuous deployment server is an enhancement of a continuous integration server that additionally deploys code to a live application environment (for example, production) if all the tests pass. It relies on automated tests to validate the entire application, so that code changes can be pushed out as fast as possible while retaining at least some semblance of quality assurance. The article *Why Continuous Deployment?* by *Eric Ries* at `http://www.startuplessonslearned.com/2009/06/why-continuous-deployment.html` is a good starting point for the motivations and practices behind continuous deployment.

Other scenarios

Test automation enables many other useful applications. For example, development utilities called **watchers** or **guards** check code periodically for modifications and perform further actions when the files change. Watchers are regularly used on a development machine to automatically run tests and display alerts when code changes have broken one or more tests, so that developers can discover errors quickly and effortlessly.

Cross-browser testing is another area made easier through automation. While a programmer can manually run a test collection on many different target browsers, this is often time consuming, error prone, and boring. Fortunately, there are testing tools that can programmatically run tests on a number of arbitrary web browsers without human interaction.

Automating browser environments

Having introduced some motivating use cases, we now turn to the nuts and bolts of automating our test infrastructure. We will cover the following techniques for programmatically driving our Backbone.js tests:

- Remote controlling tests in a real web browser
- Running tests in a browser simulation library
- Executing tests in a headless web browser environment
- Combining the first three approaches

Remote controlled web browsers

The most comprehensive automation technique is to remotely control a web browser. Remote control means that a program does what a human can do using a *real* web browser—opening the browser to a given page, clicking on links, filling in inputs, and so on.

One of the most popular remote control frameworks is **Selenium** (`http://docs.seleniumhq.org/`). Selenium provides many **web drivers**, which are programmatic adapters that hook into a real web browser and trigger actions through the normal user interface. Selenium supports a diverse array of environments, providing web drivers on different operating systems for various browsers, including Chrome, Safari, Firefox, and Internet Explorer.

> The Selenium project encompasses more features and functionality than just browser remote control. Notably, Selenium can use other test execution approaches, including headless web tools such as PhantomJS. See the Selenium projects page (`http://docs.seleniumhq.org/projects/`) and the web driver list (`http://docs.seleniumhq.org/projects/webdriver/`) for starting points and additional information.

Automating our test infrastructure with a remote control tool such as Selenium involves two basic steps: open and run the test driver page and then, infer whether or not the tests have passed. As an example, we could write a Selenium script that opens a browser window to the Notes application test driver page `notes/test/test.html` in the code samples. The Selenium script could then scrape the report page HTML to check for a telltale string such as `failures: 0` in the DOM and terminate the script with an appropriate success/failure exit code.

Thus, remote-controlled tools such as Selenium are quite powerful because they can do anything a real browser can do, just automatically. And, with a cross-platform compatible tool such as Selenium, we can run tests on nearly all modern browser/operating system combinations from a single script.

Hosted test automation providers

Capitalizing on Selenium's broad test environment support, vendors now offer services that allow users to upload a Selenium test script, designate a desired array of operating system/browser configurations, and have the service run and return test reports. One such vendor is Sauce Labs (`https://saucelabs.com/`), which runs user scripts on virtual machines with various Selenium-supported test environments. Hosted services such as these are often the quickest way to get broad browser compatibility coverage with minimum developer effort.

The remote controlled approach does have a few downsides, the first of which is that the test tools can be relatively slow. Scripts can take seconds or even minutes to hook into a target browser and run a test driver page. Additionally, these frameworks require a real web browser and a desktop windowing system. This can be an issue for build/continuous integrations that are headless, meaning they have no graphical user interface or window environment installed by default.

Simulated browser environments

An alternative automation approach is to replace the web browser with a test-friendly simulation of the browser environment and state. Typically, browser simulation libraries provide implementations of the JavaScript API within a browser such as DOM objects (for example, `window` and `document`), CSS selectors, and JSON interfaces.

JSDom (`https://github.com/tmpvar/jsdom`) is a prevalent simulation library that provides a fairly complete browser environment. JSDom is written in JavaScript and packaged as a Node.js module. Because Node.js can be easily scripted, JSDom offers us a good starting point for integrating and running Backbone.js tests from the command line.

Test automation is such a common use case that several test-friendly libraries have been written around JSDom. One such library is Zombie.js (`http://zombie.labnotes.org/`), which provides convenient browser abstractions and integration with various test frameworks, including Mocha. Using a library such as Zombie.js, we could write a Node.js script that creates a fake browser simulation, navigates to our Backbone.js test driver page, and scrapes the test result HTML to check if any tests failed. For a more in-depth treatment of testing JavaScript web applications with Zombie.js and Mocha, see *Using Node.js for UI Testing* by *Pedro Teixeira* (`http://www.packtpub.com/testing-nodejs-web-uis/book`).

Browser simulation libraries are fast because they run simulation code in the same underlying JavaScript engine as the test code without external dependencies (for example, on a real web browser executable). Simulation libraries are often quite extensible, as the simulation JavaScript code runs in the same process as the application and the tests.

However, simulations suffer from a few key drawbacks. One primary issue is that simulations can deviate from the true environment in a real web browser. Complicated browser interactions such as heavily chained event triggers or complex DOM manipulations can potentially break the simulation or behave differently than a real browser. Additionally, a browser simulation library provides only a single browser environment implementation and thus cannot test the quirks and differences across various real web browsers.

Headless web browsers

Between remote controlled browsers and simulation libraries are headless web browsers. A headless browser takes a real web browser and gets rid of the user interface, leaving only the JavaScript engine and environment. What remains is a command line tool that can navigate to web pages, execute JavaScript within the browser environment, and communicate through non-graphical interfaces such as alerts and console logging.

One of the most popular headless toolkits is PhantomJS (`http://phantomjs.org/`), which is based on the **WebKit** open source browser (`http://www.webkit.org/`) that powers browsers such as Safari. PhantomJS enhances WebKit with scripting support and a JavaScript API.

Integrating Backbone.js application tests with a headless browser is analogous to configuring a remote-controlled browser. Conveniently, PhantomJS ships with native support for a wide array of test infrastructures and offers third-party adapters for many others. See `https://github.com/ariya/phantomjs/wiki/Headless-Testing` for more test support details.

Headless web tools have a mix of some of the best features of the previous automation approaches, including the following:

- Headless JavaScript engines are often faster than remote control frameworks

- The browser environment is *real*, which avoids some of the API and correctness issues potentially found in browser simulations

- Headless frameworks are usually easy to install and can be run on servers without a windowing environment

At the same time, headless browsers incur some performance penalties from starting up and running the browser engine. They also forgo cross-browser capabilities, because headless tools are tied to a specific web browser engine implementation. Considering the overall advantages and disadvantages, headless frameworks provide a good compromise between the many mutually exclusive automation features.

Multiple environment aggregators

Capitalizing on the benefits of various approaches, many frameworks aggregate different automation schemes into a single package. For example, the following test frameworks can programmatically drive tests in major web browsers *and* PhantomJS:

- **Testem** (https://github.com/airportyh/testem)

- **Karma** (http://karma-runner.github.io/)

Aggregation frameworks are desirable because they allow a single test collection to be reused in different automation environments, although some tools are more difficult to set up and maintain than a single automation tool.

Headless testing with PhantomJS

As a concrete automation example, we will adapt our existing Backbone.js test infrastructure to use PhantomJS. PhantomJS offers an amenable set of features and capabilities for Backbone.js testing — it is fast, relatively easy to set up, and provides a real (headless) browser. As a practical matter, larger Backbone.js applications often require a real browser engine to function properly, particularly applications that exercise the murkier and more complicated parts of the browser environment.

Installing PhantomJS and the supporting tools

To get up and running with PhantomJS, let's start by installing the toolkit as per the instructions at `http://phantomjs.org/download.html`. Note that the installation procedures are operating system dependent, with packages for Windows, Mac OS X, and Linux. Alternatively, PhantomJS can be installed directly with NPM using the `phantomjs` Node.js wrapper (`https://github.com/Obvious/phantomjs`).

 We provide command line examples in this section from a UNIX-like operating system such as Linux and Mac OS X. At the same time, PhantomJS and Node.js have first class support on Windows, so the ensuing examples should be mostly analogous to what will work on Windows.

Once installation is complete, you can verify that the PhantomJS binary is available:

```
$ phantomjs --help
```

With PhantomJS in place, we next turn to the Mocha-PhantomJS bridge library. Mocha-PhantomJS uses PhantomJS to run a Mocha test driver page and transform the test results into formatted command line output. The library throws proper errors on test failures, making it quite useful for scripting. See the online documentation at `http://metaskills.net/mocha-phantomjs/` for additional capabilities and details.

To install Mocha-PhantomJS, you need the Node.js framework, which can be obtained by following the instructions at `http://nodejs.org/download/`. A modern Node.js installation includes the NPM package manager tool used for Mocha-PhantomJS. We can confirm that Node.js and the package manager are correctly installed with the following commands:

```
$ node --help
```
```
$ npm --help
```

Next, install Mocha-PhantomJS with the global NPM flag (`-g`) to make the `mocha-phantomjs` binary available anywhere in a shell:

```
$ npm install -g mocha-phantomjs
```

After NPM finishes the installation, check whether Mocha-PhantomJS is available with the following command:

```
$ mocha-phantomjs --help
```

Running Backbone.js tests with PhantomJS

With the necessary tools installed, we can now adapt our Backbone.js test infrastructure to run against PhantomJS. Mocha-PhantomJS provides a replacement proxy object, `mochaPhantomJS`, to control Mocha tests and reports. We just need to replace the real `mocha` object where `mocha.run()` is normally called in the test driver web page. Inserting the following code snippet into the test driver page will allow Mocha to run *both* in a real browser and with PhantomJS:

```
<!-- Test Setup -->
<script>
  var expect = chai.expect;
  mocha.setup("bdd");

  window.onload = function () {
    (window.mochaPhantomJS || mocha).run();
  };
</script>
```

Once we have modified the test driver page with the `(window.mochaPhantomJS || mocha).run()` function call, we can execute the page tests with Mocha-PhantomJS. For example, if we modify the Notes application test driver file `chapters/05/test/test.html` from the previous chapter with the `mochaPhantomJS` change, we can run the file and generate the following command line report:

```
$ mocha-phantomjs chapters/05/test/test.html


  App.Views.NotesItem
    remove
      √ is removed on model destroy
    render
      √ renders on model change w/ stub
      √ renders on model change w/ mock
    DOM
      √ renders data to HTML
    actions
      √ views on click
      √ edits on click
      √ deletes on click
```

```
App.Routers.Router
  √ can route to note
  √ can route around


9 tests complete (39 ms)
```

Reviewing this report, we can see that all of our tests passed, and that the PhantomJS test run was quite fast, clocking in at 39 milliseconds. With these modest test driver web page changes, we can run nearly any test web page from the command line or a build script using PhantomJS.

Automating tests in the code samples

Putting these suggested principles into practice, nearly all of the test code samples presented in this book are scripted to run from the command line under PhantomJS. If you review the downloadable code samples repository, you will notice that all of the chapter and application test pages actually use the (window.mochaPhantomJS || mocha).run() function call instead of a raw mocha.run() statement.

The integration of PhantomJS into the code samples provides a practical starting point for some of the automated testing use cases that we discussed earlier in this chapter. Specifically, the examples implement the following automation scenarios:

- **Command line tests**: The code samples contain a Node.js NPM package. json file with script commands that can run chapter and application test driver pages with PhantomJS.

- **Continuous integration server**: The GitHub repository for the code samples (https://github.com/ryan-roemer/backbone-testing/) uses the Travis continuous integration server for automated failure alerts. Travis is configured to run all of the example tests with PhantomJS on every code change. Travis is a particularly good choice for a test infrastructure such as the one presented in this book because its build environment already contains PhantomJS and it is quite amenable to Node.js and NPM modules such as Mocha-PhantomJS. To see all of this in action, you can navigate a browser to https://travis-ci. org/ryan-roemer/backbone-testing at any time to check out the live build status for all of the code we have discussed in this book. (Hopefully you will find that all of our tests are passing!)

Parting thoughts, next steps, and future ideas

We are now at the end of our journey through the fundamentals of testing Backbone.js applications with Mocha, Chai, and Sinon.JS. We have explored the background, configuration, and use of each of these test frameworks and tried out a number of complementary tools and helpers. We have reviewed Backbone.js application development, specific component testing goals, and written test collections around a full Backbone.js application. So, what comes next?

Our first suggestion is to review the online documentation for the various testing technologies. The official APIs and guides for all of the frameworks we use in the book are quite good and can provide starting points for more complicated test scenarios that may arise in real-world Backbone.js application development. As a refresher, the documentation sites for our core test stack include the following:

- **Mocha**: `http://visionmedia.github.io/mocha/`
- **Chai**: `http://chaijs.com/`
- **Sinon.JS**: `http://sinonjs.org/`

After the framework documentation, you can review the article, blog, and book suggestions that we have provided throughout this book. In particular, the references in *Chapter 2, Creating a Backbone.js Application Test Plan* on general test methodology and Backbone.js testing are great resources for those seeking a broader background in the software development and testing techniques appropriate for larger-scale Backbone.js applications.

Finally, we suggest that you download and install the book code samples. These samples are essentially the practical application of the principles we have covered in this book, with useful applications, tests, and files put together in a single package. Additionally, they provide examples of more testing and automation techniques for you to explore on your own, including the following:

- **Style checking**: JavaScript style checkers automatically analyze source files to find language or convention errors. Checkers are invaluable during software development, often finding programming errors early on and in places that tests can miss. Additionally, style checkers can enforce consistent coding styles for all members of a team working on a single application. The code samples use JSHint (`http://www.jshint.com/`) to check all of the application and test examples that we have discussed in this book. You can inspect the `package.json` file in the code samples to see our JSHint usage in the script commands `style`, `style-server`, and `style-client`.

- **Code coverage**: Code coverage is a technique to quantify how much of an application is actually exercised by tests. Coverage tools run behind the scenes during tests, recording which application code lines are executed, and provide a report that measures the lines covered in each application file. The code samples provide a test driver page for the Notes application at `notes/test/coverage.html` that uses **Blanket.js** (`http://blanketjs.org/`) to provide a coverage report. You can run the Notes test and the coverage report online at `http://backbone-testing.com/notes/test/coverage.html`.

The rest is left up to you. While we are at the end of the road for this book, the world of testing will keep pushing forward in new and interesting ways. We bid you good luck in your continued learning and discovery of more testing tools, methods, and topics for Backbone.js application development.

Summary

In this chapter, we have learned how to remove manual browser interaction from the test process with an introduction to test automation approaches and use cases. We have investigated different tools to drive our tests from the command line and worked through a concrete test automation implementation using PhantomJS to drive our Backbone.js application tests.

Also, we left with a few final thoughts on the principles that we have developed throughout the course of this book and where to turn next. Hopefully, you now have the fundamentals and direction to create your own Backbone.js test infrastructures, apply good test-driven application development practices, and tackle your frontend tests with confidence.

Index

test() 48
function spies 82

G

GitHub 138
grep feature 18
guards 138

H

headless testing, PhantomJS 142
headless web browsers 141, 142
hosted test automation providers 140
HTML fixtures
  creating, for view tests 68
Hulu 7

I

installation, Chai plugins 88
installation, PhantomJS 143
it() function 47

J

Jasmine 12
Jenkins
  about 138
  URL 138
jQuery
  about 8
  URL 8
JSDom
  about 140
  URL 140
JSHint 146

K

Karma
  URL 142

L

language chain objects, Chai
  about 51
  deep 51
  not 51

LinkedIn 7
list item view
  about 121, 122
  testing 122-125
Local Application 26

M

menu bar view
  about 92, 93
  spying 93-96
  testing 93-96
method behaviors
  replacing, with Sinon.JS stubs 110
Mocha
  about 10, 11
  BDD interface 47
  need for 12
  TDD interface 48
  test interfaces 46
  URL 146
Mocha BDD interface
  about 47
  functional units 47
Mocha TDD interface 48
Mocha test interfaces
  Behavior-Driven Development (BDD) 46
  exports 46
  QUnit-styled 46
  Test-Driven Development (TDD) 46
Mocha test runner 56
Mocha test specifications
  writing 61
mock API 115
mock.expects(methodName) method 115
mock.restore() method 115
mocks
  about 13, 80, 114
  Backbone.js components, testing 117-119
  behavior, faking with 114
  behavior, verifying with 114
mock.verify() method 115
models 24, 35
Model-View-Controller (MVC) 24
MongoDB
  URL 133
multiple environment aggregators 142

N

Node.js Express
  URL 133
Notes application
  about 27, 28
  anatomy 28-31
  components, searching 130, 131
  router, testing 125-128
Notes application single note view 66-68
Notes list item view 120, 121
Notes menu bar view
  about 91-93
  spying 93-96
  testing 93-96
Notes single note view
  about 96-99
  testing 100-106

O

object method spies 83
objects
  chaining 50
object validation, Chai 53, 54

P

partial integrations 37
partial integration tests 34
performance/load tests 34
PhantomJS
  about 10, 139, 141
  Backbone.js tests, running with 144, 145
  headless testing 142
  installing 143
  URL 141
project style
  deciding 49

Q

QUnit-styled interface 46
QUnit test framework
  URL 46

R

regression tests 34
remote backend
  faking, in Backbone.js application 133-135
remote controlled web browsers 139, 140
restore() function 83
router routes 119
routers
  about 25, 37
  testing, in Notes application 125-128
router tests
  running 128, 129

S

Safari 141
sandbox 84
Sauce Labs
  about 140
  URL 140
Selenium
  about 139, 140
  URL 139
Server Application 26
server.respond() method 132
server.respondWith(method, url, response)
      method 132
server.respondWith(response) method 132
server.restore() method 133
setTimeout() function 19, 84
setup() function 56
setup() method 48
Showdown 29
simulated browser environments 140, 141
single note view
  about 97-100
  testing 100-106
Sinon-Chai plugin 88
sinon.fakeServer.create() method 132
Sinon.JS
  about 10, 13, 79, 81, 109
  asynchronous callbacks, in stubbed
        methods 112
  spy API 85

testing
  application, reconfiguring for 56, 57
testing and automation techniques
  about 146
  code coverage 147
  style checking 146
test interfaces, Mocha
  Behavior-Driven Development (BDD) 46
  exports 46
  QUnit-styled 46
  Test-Driven Development (TDD) 46
test libraries
  Chai 12
  Mocha 11
  obtaining 10-13
  Sinon.JS 13
test() method 48
test methods 32
test paradigms 32
test plan 33
test report
  about 16
  actions 17
test repository structure
  designing 9, 10
test results
  assessing 16, 17
  running 16, 17
tests
  adding 15
  asynchronous behavior 61
  automating, in code samples 145
  orgainizing 55
  setting up 13
  starting up 59, 61
  winding down 59, 61
  writing 13
test speed 18-20
test style
  selecting 45
throw assertion 55
TodoMVC
  URL 31
topics
  test code, organizing into 58

Travis
  about 138
  URL 138

U

Underscore.js
  about 8
  URL 8
unit tests 33
usability tests 34
USA Today 7
utilities 37

V

value assertions, Chai 51, 52
view events 119
views
  about 25, 36
  running 128, 129
  supporting 65
view tests
  hooking up 106, 107
  HTML fixtures, creating for 68
  running 106, 107
view test suite 69-71

W

watchers 138
web drivers 139
WebKit
  about 141
  URL 141

X

XMLHttpRequest (XHR) 132

Z

Zombie.js
  about 141
  URL 141

Thank you for buying
Backbone.js Testing

About Packt Publishing

Packt, pronounced 'packed', published its first book "*Mastering phpMyAdmin for Effective MySQL Management*" in April 2004 and subsequently continued to specialize in publishing highly focused books on specific technologies and solutions.

Our books and publications share the experiences of your fellow IT professionals in adapting and customizing today's systems, applications, and frameworks. Our solution based books give you the knowledge and power to customize the software and technologies you're using to get the job done. Packt books are more specific and less general than the IT books you have seen in the past. Our unique business model allows us to bring you more focused information, giving you more of what you need to know, and less of what you don't.

Packt is a modern, yet unique publishing company, which focuses on producing quality, cutting-edge books for communities of developers, administrators, and newbies alike. For more information, please visit our website: www.packtpub.com.

About Packt Open Source

In 2010, Packt launched two new brands, Packt Open Source and Packt Enterprise, in order to continue its focus on specialization. This book is part of the Packt Open Source brand, home to books published on software built around Open Source licences, and offering information to anybody from advanced developers to budding web designers. The Open Source brand also runs Packt's Open Source Royalty Scheme, by which Packt gives a royalty to each Open Source project about whose software a book is sold.

Writing for Packt

We welcome all inquiries from people who are interested in authoring. Book proposals should be sent to author@packtpub.com. If your book idea is still at an early stage and you would like to discuss it first before writing a formal book proposal, contact us; one of our commissioning editors will get in touch with you.

We're not just looking for published authors; if you have strong technical skills but no writing experience, our experienced editors can help you develop a writing career, or simply get some additional reward for your expertise.

Selenium Testing Tools Cookbook

ISBN: 978-1-84951-574-0   Paperback: 326 pages

Over 90 recipes to build, maintain, and improve test automation with Selenium WebDriver

1. Learn to leverage the power of Selenium WebDriver with simple examples that illustrate real world problems and their workarounds

2. Each sample demonstrates key concepts allowing you to advance your knowledge of Selenium WebDriver in a practical and incremental way

3. Explains testing of mobile web applications with Selenium Drivers for platforms such as iOS and Android

BackTrack 5 Cookbook

ISBN: 978-1-84951-738-6   Paperback: 296 pages

Over 80 recipes to execute many of the best known and little known penetration testing aspects of BackTrack 5

1. Learn to perform penetration tests with BackTrack 5

2. Nearly 100 recipes designed to teach penetration testing principles and build knowledge of BackTrack 5 Tools

3. Provides detailed step-by-step instructions on the usage of many of BackTrack's popular and not-so- popular tools

Please check **www.PacktPub.com** for information on our titles